"I used these ideas in class and had a wonderful day with my students."

Thank you so much!! I used these ideas in class and had a wonderful day with my students. As a first Year Relief Teacher I find this site invaluable in helping me become a better and more confident Teacher.

Jess (Take Control of the Noisy Class customer)

* * *

"It is very rewarding to see a teacher apply strategies from Rob's materials, then get excited as they see the 'magic' work."

"The materials have been right on target, students have benefitted as well as teachers. It is very rewarding to see a teacher apply strategies from Rob's materials, then get excited as they see the 'magic' work. Thank you for making my job easier and validating the experience."

Cheryl E. Le Fon (Take Control of the Noisy Class customer)

The Fun Teacher's Tool kit

Hundreds of Ways to Create a Positive Classroom Environment & Make Learning FUN

Needs-Focused Teaching Resource Book 4

Rob Plevin

www.needsfocusedteaching.com

About the Author

Rob Plevin is an ex-deputy head teacher and Special Education Teacher with the practical experience to help teachers in today's toughest classrooms.

No stranger to behaviour management issues, Rob was 'asked to leave' school as a teenager. Despite his rocky route through the education system he managed to follow his dream of becoming a teacher after spending several years working as an outdoor instructor, corporate trainer and youth worker for young people in crisis. Since then he has worked with challenging young people in residential settings, care units and tough schools and was most recently employed as Deputy Head at a PRU for children and teenagers with behaviour problems. He was identified as a key player in the team which turned the unit round from 'Special Measures'.

He now runs needsfocusedteaching.com, is the author of several books and presents training courses internationally for teachers, lecturers, parents and care workers on behaviour management & motivation. His live courses are frequently described as 'unforgettable' and he was rated as an 'outstanding' teacher by the UK's Office for Standards in Education.

Rob's courses and resources feature the Needs-Focused Approach™ – a very effective system for preventing and dealing with behaviour problems in which positive staff/student relationships are given highest priority.

To book Rob for INSET or to enquire about live training please visit the help desk at

www.needsfocusedteaching.com

Introduction

Free bonus materials & printable resources

This book, like the others in this series, is for teachers like you who want to connect and succeed with tough, hard-to-reach students in the shortest possible time. To help you do this, it comes complete with additional bonus material as well as printable resources to accompany the activities explained in the book.

 Wherever you see the **'resource icon'** in this book, head over to our website to get your free resources and accompanying printables,

Please visit:

http://needsfocusedteaching.com/kindle/fun/

About the Book

The FUN Teacher's Tool Kit is book #4 in my Needs-Focused Teaching Resource series. This collection of teaching books is my attempt to provide teachers with practical, fast-acting, tried-and-tested strategies and resources that work like magic in today's toughest schools. The novel, quirky ideas and methods form part of my Needs Focused Approach and have been tried and tested with hard-to-reach, reluctant learners of all ages, in more than 40 countries. Over the last 10 years or more they have been found to be highly effective in improving learning, raising achievement, building trusting relationships and creating positive learning environments.

Each book in this series includes a comprehensive suite of bonus materials and printable resources as I want to give you as much support as possible and for you to be delighted with your book purchase. Please be sure to download your bonus resources from my website here:

http://needsfocusedteaching.com/kindle/fun/

The Needs Focused Approach

The Needs-Focused Teaching System is explained fully in my main classroom management book, 'Take Control of the Noisy Class – From Chaos to Calm in 15 seconds'. It's available on Amazon in both Kindle and physical formats.

Briefly, this approach is based on Abraham Maslow's Hierarchy of Needs theory which suggests that human beings share a wide range of emotional and psychological needs – from the need to achieve through the need to contribute, to the need for love and a whole host of others in between.

By meeting these needs in the classroom teachers can effectively maximise student engagement while preventing behaviour problems which often arise due to feelings of boredom, frustration and alienation. We focus on just three broad groups - 'Empowerment' which includes things like recognition, freedom, autonomy, achievement, contribution, choice and competence; 'Fun' which includes curiosity, interest, growth and learning, adventure, amusement, surprise, variety; and finally the need to 'Belong' – to be accepted, valued, appreciated, needed, related to or connected with something beyond oneself.

The ideas and activities in this book will help you give your students a sense of belonging – by making them feel part of the classroom community, by strengthening peer relationships and by building positive, mutually respectful student-teacher bonds. They will help you empower your students by providing them with realistic chances to achieve and experience success, by giving them a degree of autonomy and choice and by ensuring their efforts are recognised and acknowledged. And they will help you improve motivation in lessons by providing opportunities to have fun.

The various games, fun fill-ins, energisers and ideas in The Fun Teacher's Tool Kit can be used for virtually any lesson topic or subject area to enliven the subject and deepen learning and retention through cooperative interaction and kinesthetic learning.

Classroom Games

Every teacher can benefit by having a range of games up his or her sleeve to use in the classroom. Over the past 6 years running training courses for teachers I have asked the question, "Why do you think it is important to use games in the classroom?" And from the feedback I've received I've constructed the following list of the very best reasons. Hopefully this list will encourage you to use games more often in your own lessons, if you're not already doing so...

Reason #1: Games Make learning Fun

Games bring fun and energy into a learning zone by engaging players, motivating them to interact with the topic and linking positive emotions to the learning process. Learners are able to demonstrate their understanding of a topic in a friendly contest where successes are memorable moments of shared triumph and celebration and where mistakes are not seen as a personal weakness. And because the game format is playful, the inherent challenge of the material, (even new or difficult material), is less threatening.

Reason #2: Games improve learning

Games often appeal to different learning styles and involve both the rational and experiential mind that helps players remember what they have learned. They provide an environment that transforms the passive student into an active part of the learning process.

Reason #3: Games Provide Feedback to the Learner

Like jokes, games give immediate feedback on performance in an acceptable way. If people laugh when you tell a joke, you've been successful; when you take part in a game, successes and errors give feedback as to the quality of your participation and input. With the appropriate corrective feedback from the teacher, games can become an invaluable learning opportunity.

Reason #4: Games Build a Sense of Belonging, Develop Positive Staff/student & Student/Student Relationships and Develop the Class 'Community'

Games bring players into teams and demonstrate the rules and roles of working together and getting on with others as part of a team. They also give your learners a chance to interact closely with their peers as they share the highs and lows of the game experience, allowing for strong bonding and community-building.

Reason #5: Games Help Teach Social Skills.

This is an incredibly important point. Games provide an arena where social skills can be learned and practiced. We can't 'tell' a person to have better social skills and we can't 'make' them get on with other people. They have to learn for themselves the benefits of doing so. Students soon learn that the only way they will be able to participate in a fun activity or game is by playing to the rules or using appropriate social skills which they are then able to draw on in a variety of real-life situations.

Classroom Game 1:

'Bingo'

Overview: This game follows the format of the traditional game, Bingo and is a surprisingly engaging and well-received activity.

Materials:

•Prepare a list of terms and definitions. To make 5x5 square bingo cards, you'll need 25-35 terms.

•Input the terms into a Random Bingo Card Generator, like this one:

(http://print-bingo.com)

Or make up your own cards using the simple template in the online resource section which accompanies this guide, here:

http://needsfocusedteaching.com/kindle/fun/

- One card for each student.

- Tokens to cover squares on the Bingo cards

Time: Approx. 10 minutes (Can be extended into a longer activity. The first time this is played it may take longer than ten minutes. Once participants know what to do they can be encouraged to work through quite fast).

Directions:

1. Each student has a card with a grid showing terms/answers related to the lesson content (as explained above)

2. The teacher reads off definitions and if students have a term that matches that definition, they cover the corresponding square with a token. Students "win" when they get a line of 5 squares (or, alternately, the entire board) covered.

TIP:

A very quick and easy way to run this game with minimum preparation is to provide each person with a blank grid – or even get them to draw their own – with 6 spaces. Write up on the board 30 terms/keywords/ answers associated with the lesson topic and get them to pick any six to put in the spaces on their grid.

Classroom Game 2:

'Memory Game'

Overview:

This is a particularly good game for low-level memory tasks such as terms and definitions and is great for waking students up in the middle of a lesson.

Number of people: Can be played individually, in pairs, in small groups or as a whole class activity.

Materials:

- Sets of separate question/answer cards.

- Vary the types of cards you create:

  questions/answers,

  terms/definitions,

  images/labels,

  if/then statements,

  true/false statements,

  date/event pairs etc.

Time: Approx. 10-15 minutes

Directions:

Cards are placed face-down on the table or stuck to the board. Students flip over two cards at a time. If the cards make a pair, they take those cards off the board and go again. If the cards don't make a pair, they flip the cards face-down again and the next student tries.

Note:

If played with the whole class, sticking the cards on the board with 'Blu-tac®' and having students come up to the board to make their selections adds more activity to the game and suits kinesthetic learners.

Classroom Game 3:

'Taboo'

Overview:

Word guessing game made famous by the board game creator, Hasbro. The objective of the game is for a player to have his/her teammates guess the word on his/her card without using the word itself or additional 9Taboo) words listed on the card. Very easily adapted for any subject topic.

Number of people: Can be played in pairs, in small groups or as a whole class activity.

Materials:

Sets of 'Taboo' question cards. These can be adapted for curriculum use (see below for a simple Math example), buzzer, timer

Time: Approx. 10-15 minutes (Can be extended into a longer activity.)

Directions:

1. Players take turns as the 'Speaker'. The Speaker attempts to prompt his or her teammates to guess as many keywords as possible in the allotted time.

2. On each card is a list of "taboo" (forbidden) words which may not be spoken.

3. Should the speaker say a Taboo word, a 'Moderator'on the opposing team sounds a buzzer (if you have one) and the speaker must move on to the next word.

4. The speaker can only use speech to prompt his or her teammates; gestures, sounds or drawings are not allowed. The speaker's hints may not rhyme with a Taboo word, or be an abbreviation of a Taboo word.

5. Once the team correctly guesses the word exactly as written on the card, the giver moves on to the next word, trying to get as many words as possible in the allotted time.

6. When time runs out, play passes to the next adjacent player of the other team. The playing team receives one point for correct guesses and one penalty point if "taboo" words are spoken.

Classroom Game 4:

'Odd One Out'

Overview:

Students are given groups of words or pictures and have to decide which one is different from the others. Very easy to adapt to different ability levels and subjects.

Number of people: Can be played individually, in pairs, in small groups or as a whole class activity.

Materials:

Groups of Odd One Out pictures and/or words – presented either on cards, worksheets or as slides on a whiteboard.

Time: Approx. 10-15 minutes (Can be extended into a longer activity.

Directions:

1. Whole class activity: Players are given a response sheet; questions are flashed on the whiteboard for each student to work on individually in a given time period

2. Teams/pairs activity: As above but teams/pairs work together to complete their response sheet

Tip:

Teams/partners can be given time to create cards for opposing teams based on their subject knowledge.

Example 1:

A. Tokyo

B. Sydney

C. New York

D. Brazil

Answer: D (a country, not a city)

Example 2:

A. Sasha slept all day yesterday

B. Paul is working at the hotel

C. Tony is washing his car

D. We are walking as fast as we can

Answer: A (Past tense)

'Just a Minute'

Overview:

Classroom version of the popular radio show of the same name. Very easy to adapt to different ability levels and subjects.

Number of people: Up to 40. Can be played in small groups or as a whole class activity.

Materials:

Timer, buzzer and topic suggestions on individual cards

Time: Approx. 10-15 minutes (Can be extended into a longer activity.

Directions:

1. Divide class into two or more teams

2. Students from each team take turns to take a topic card and then try to talk about that topic for 60 seconds. (For lower ability or younger students start with 30 seconds)

3. The speaker can be 'challenged' by the opposing team based on the following rules:

    i.   Hesitation - the easiest challenge, awarded if the speaker 'erms' or 'ums'.

    ii. Repetition - the speaker is not allowed to repeat any words or phrases which are not contained in the topic title itself. Pronouns, prepositions etc. can obviously be repeated.

    iii. Deviation - Best only used with older/more capable groups. A challenge can be lodged if the speaker goes off the given topic.

4. Points can be awarded by an 'adjudicator' as follows:

- 2 points for a speaker who manages to speak for the allotted time

- 1 point for a correct challenge

- 1 point for surviving a challenge (if a challenge is deemed incorrect by the adjudicator, the speaker keeps the topic and carries on speaking).

5. Play passes over to opposing team if challenge is accepted by 'adjudicator'.

Classroom Game 6:

'Non-Stop Talker'

Overview:

Fast-paced, fun game in which a student tries to get his/her team mates to say every keyword on a list within a time limit. Very easy to adapt to different ability levels and curriculum topics.

Number of people: Up to 40. Can be played in small groups or as a whole class activity.

Materials:

Timer, buzzer and 'Keyword Cards'

Time: Approx. 10-15 minutes (Can be extended into a longer activity.

Directions:

1. Divide class into two or more teams

2. A speaker from each team has to describe or mime each keyword for his or her team members

3. Each team is given 60 seconds to try and say each word on their speaker's 'Keyword Card'

4. Points are awarded as follows:

- 3 Points if all words are stated within 30 seconds

- 2 points if all words are stated within 45 seconds

- 1 points if all words are stated within 60 seconds

5. Play passes to the opposing team/s in turn after each 1 minute play period

Classroom Game 7:

'Sequence Ball'

Overview:

A simple, active game in which students use a ball to mark the steps in a sequence or process

Number of people: Up to 40 – usually played individually

Materials:

A foam ball or bean bag (Bean bags have the advantage of being less 'bouncy')

Time: Approx. 10-15 minutes (Can be extended into a longer activity.

Directions:

1. One student says the first letter of a word or the first step in a sequence etc. and then throws the ball to someone else who has to say the next letter, next step etc.

Classroom Game 8:

'Flashcard Relay'

Overview:

A fast and furious relay game suitable for small groups

Number of people: Up to 20 – usually played in small teams of 3-4

Materials:

Pre-written question/answer cards, clear space on two classroom walls

Time: Approx. 10-15 minutes (Can be extended into a longer activity).

Directions:

1. Teacher prepares question/answer cards as follows: Write individual terms or questions on a set of index cards and the definitions or answers on another set. The 'Question Cards' are taped on one room wall, and the 'Answer Cards' on the opposite wall.

2. One student from each team must run & grab a term or 'Question Card' and then the matching definition or 'Answer Card'.

3. If the student picks up a match, the team gets a point, and the next team member gets to go. The team with the most points at the end of the game wins.

Classroom Game 9:

'Flipchart Fight'

Overview:

Teams of students compete in a fun, active duel or relay to create a content-related acrostic or similar puzzle in this quick-and-easy-to-set up game

Number of people: Up to 40 – usually played in teams of 4-5

Materials: Sugar/flip chart paper for each team, timer.

Time: Approx. 10-15 minutes (Can be extended into a longer activity).

Directions:

1. Teacher writes or calls out a topic word.

2. A member from each team writes the topic word down the left side of their flipchart or sugar paper in bold/coloured letters and pins their paper on a wall in the classroom

3. Team members stand opposite their piece of sugar paper on the other side of the room

4. When the time starts, team members take it in turns to run to their paper and add one word to their acrostic/puzzle before handing the pen to the next player in their team

5. The winning team is the first to complete their puzzle

NB// For more classroom games see the bonus book 'Classroom Games' which you'll find in the online resource area here:

http://needsfocusedteaching.com/kindle/fun/

More Fun Ideas

Puppets & Ventriloquists' Dolls

Puppets are not only a great way to add humour to lessons - they can also help teach social skills, solve disagreements and enhance learning with any age group. Here are some ways to use puppets and ventriloquist dolls in your lessons...

1. Use specific puppets or dolls to teach the topic that they relate to

The puppet can deliver an introduction, perform a demonstration, act as 'host' for a class quiz, take part in a Q & A or 'Ask the Expert' session etc.

- A doctor or nurse puppet can teach about human biology, diet, vitamins etc

- A 'mad scientist' puppet can teach science

- A farmer puppet can teach about the environment

- An alien puppet can teach about planets and the solar system

- Puppets from different countries or religious groups can talk about their life and beliefs

2. Use puppets as a classroom management aid

Young children often respond much more easily and positively to requests from a puppet. A puppet can also provide much-needed humour in highly charged, emotional situations. Think 'Mr Punch'.

3. Use puppets to solve disagreements between students

A puppet can be a very effective mediator in restorative practices asking questions such as:

- What happened?

- What were you thinking?

- How were you feeling?

- Who else has been affected by this?

- What do you need now so that the problem can be resolved?

4. Use puppets to develop students' presentation and social skills

It can be far less daunting for a student to make a presentation by speaking 'through' or 'to' a puppet. Similarly, social skills can be practiced by 'acting out' or role-playing and using a puppet as one of the characters.

Props

Props are a great way to keep the attention of your students; they have two main uses. They can be funny - such as an Elvis wig or clown's nose - to amuse and entertain, keep the mood upbeat and break the monotony of teacher-talk and demonstrations. Or they can be used as an aid to learning to make explanations easier to understand, focus attention and demonstrate abstract concepts in a visual and concrete way.. And now, here's our list of props you shouldn't be without...

14 Must-Have Props for Teachers

1. Pictures

Clips from magazines and newspapers, print-outs from computers, poster images and real-life photos relating to your subject can all be used to test assumptions, illustrate a point or spark discussion. A single photograph could be used for a wide variety of activities and as a source for almost limitless questions using 'who', 'what', 'where', 'when', 'why' & 'how' as a basis.

"Describe what is happening in the picture"

"What do you think happened next?"

"What was being said by this person?"

"How do you think this person is feeling and why?"

"Where is this happening?"

"When is this happening?"

2. Coloured Markers

No teacher should be without a full range of coloured markers for flip chart/board work. They help students associate key points with visual references. For example, in language teaching, colours can be linked with certain tenses, structures or functions. The most important point to remember when using coloured chalk or markers is to be consistent.

If you use green for past tenses in an explanation or demonstration, try to always use green for past tenses from that point on.

3. Audio and video recorders

Audio and video recorders are traditionally used to present listening and/or visual learning materials to students. I once started an enjoyable lesson on adjectives with a recording of my elderly father saying just two words... "very nice" ...in his broad Cheshire accent. It was a novel little starter – the kids immediately wanted to know who it was on the recording and why I was playing it. Job done, I had their attention.

A story followed about how I'd heard my dad say those same two words to my mum after every evening meal as I was growing up. No variation, just the same words, "very nice", no matter how delicious the meal was, no matter how much time and effort had gone into it.

We then discussed as a class how he could have substituted other words instead of 'very' and 'nice' to convey his feelings – such as 'absolutely delicious' etc. We then looked through a thesaurus to generate more ideas and, as the main task, each student produced a 'prompt sheet' of suitable phrases for my dad to use next time he sat down for a meal!

Here are a few other suggestions for using either a voice or video player/recorder in lessons:

A. **Have students record their conversations as they explain key points to each other.** The feedback involved is invaluable - and often more effective than simple teacher correction. Students are surprisingly quick to catch their own mistakes in when listening to themselves on tape.

B. **Have students practice and prepare a presentation or dialogue for a video or voice recording.** Students preparing materials for a finished "project" tend to be very involved in that project. This involvement contributes to effective "long-term" learning.

C. **Have groups of students film 'Adverts', 'News shows', 'Interview with an expert' or 'Instructional videos' as projects for the current unit of study.** This can be a bit painful for shy students, but the learning that accomplished is impressive and it often uncovers some amazing talent.

4. Hats, wigs and face props (beards, glasses etc.)

Use these props to help students immediately get into their roles during role-play sessions or when using 'Response dice' (see below).

5. 'In the style of...' Dice

 These can be used at any stage of a lesson during question/answer phases to inject some humour and develop confidence in students. There's a template in your resource area, online here:

http://needsfocusedteaching.com/kindle/fun/

Simply ask students to either respond in a nominated style (see below) or roll the 'In the style of..' die.

Suggested styles:

- Newsreader

- Monk (Gregorian chant)

- Builder

- Dracula

- Very happy person (lottery/speedboat winner)

- Miserable person (lottery loser)

- Angry person (lottery winner who has had his/her ticket stolen)

- Very boring person

- Superhero

- Farmer

- Mad scientist

- Weather girl/man

- Pilot

- Rock Star

- Children's TV presenter

- Mime

6. Feedback Signs

Give a 'Good Answer' sign to a student at the front of the room. During discussions and Q&A sessions, when a student responds with a good answer, point to the student who has the sign and get them to hold it up for everyone to see. Variations include 'Well done', 'Try again', 'Outstanding!' etc.

7. Sponge hands

Give students sponge hand shapes or card cut-outs on the end of sticks to 'raise' instead of their hand when they want to ask a question or respond with an answer.

8. Hooters, horns, whistles, bells and kazoos

These are great for alerting students to finish an activity, warn them one is coming to an end or signify the start one. They are also fun to use during quizzes and Q & A sessions – a bell for a right answer, a duck call for a wrong answer and a hooter for 'times up'. I have a colleague who has downloaded a sound effects application for his iPhone and plugs it in to speakers during lessons. Just about any sound you can think of is available and, used sparingly, can be hilarious.

9. Awards and trophies

Awards are almost always used in classrooms in the form of certificates but why stop there? A trophy is far more appealing – even if it is just a flimsy, plastic joke 'Oscar' – and it doesn't have to be something they take home, it's the recognition and the ceremony that counts. A very brief, simple award ceremony can take place at the end of a lesson or once a month/term to highlight students' progress in any given area.

Today's 'Independent Worker' award goes to...

Today's 'Early Finisher' award goes to...

Today's 'Most Improved Student' is...

Today's 'Mrs Mop' award for tidying the room goes to...

Today's 'Mr Motivator' award for keeping everyone positive goes to...

10. Team hats, badges & flags

Team hats, logos, badges and table flags help create a sense of unity and team spirit.

11. Clapper board

Use for role plays, for drawing attention to excellent work or to stop an activity to give feedback.

12. Teacher's mortar board and gown

Ideal when students are involved in a peer-teaching role.

13. Subject-related props

Without doubt the best prop I ever had the privilege to use in a lesson was a genuine relic from the Titanic. It was a broken pocket watch belonging to a young boy who had been working as a Bell Boy on one of the lifts before he tragically drowned. My students had been working on their research project for a few weeks and were fascinated by the whole Titanic story. To see this piece of living history up-close, after previously only having access to pictures, videos and reference books, was simply amazing for them. They had already discovered the exact time the ship was documented as taking her final plunge - 2:20am – and had filled this time in as the last entry on their time lines. When they saw that the watch had actually stopped at precisely 2:20am, they were, understandably, completely spellbound. It was a tremendous example of how powerful props can be.

Obviously this was a one-off. The chances of getting your hands on priceless relics are slim and any efforts to procure them from your local museum may not be viewed favourably. I was lucky – a friend of mine knew the lady who owned the watch (and several other artefacts). She had never shown them to anyone outside her home up to that point but was thrilled to be able to enhance the children's education by coming in to school to display them. Like I say, I was lucky, but we all have friends and relatives and it's possible that one of them has, or knows someone who has, a suitable prop for your next lesson.

Subject-related props can literally bring a subject to life. As an introduction to a lesson they can grab attention like nothing else. The Titanic watch, for example, was actually introduced to the group as part of one of the activities from another book in this series (Attention Grabbing Starters and Plenaries) – 'What's in the bag?'

When the students entered the room, the bag (one of the original sacks used by the authorities to hold passengers' belongings retrieved after the accident) was waiting ominously on a table in the middle of the room. They were instantaneously attracted to it and were desperate to find out what it was. Job done; we had their attention.

14. Dice

Here are some ideas for the use of dice in class.

a. For giving choices involving a range of activities

(e.g. six choices on the board – Cloze exercise, Mind-map, Newspaper report, Poster, Text book, practical activity etc.)

b. For selecting random group members for cooperative work

c. For adding humour to Q & A sessions

Put up six response styles on the board e.g. 'Old person', 'Rock star', 'Farmer', 'News reporter', 'Mad scientist', 'Salesman'. When students are asked to give feedback or answer questions they must do so on the style chosen by their throw of the dice. (Alternatively, the choices could be six famous TV/music personalities for students to impersonate as they give their answer).

d. For adding novelty and humour to humdrum routines

Break the "routine habit" and add an element of novelty to routine classroom activities. For example – ask the class "How shall I take the register today?" and elicit 6 options e.g. 'Happily', 'angrily', 'from the back of the room', 'in a French accent', 'without moving my lips' etc.

Mindbenders, Puzzles & Riddles

I've used puzzles in the classroom throughout my teaching career and I've noticed several positive effects both on the students themselves and the classroom environment as a whole such as:

1. There are often fewer behaviour problems. I suppose one of the reasons for this is because students are never bored – there is always something for them to do. Whenever Jonny needs five minutes to re-focus himself, the challenge of a puzzle is often enough to settle him back down.

2. There is an increased sense of community in the classroom. Particularly where physical puzzles are concerned (metal and wooden puzzles), students have ownership – these are their puzzles for their class to try out and solve. They enjoy having a range of puzzles they can pick up, hold and try to solve and they enjoy the challenge of seeing who can solve the most difficult.

The great thing is that puzzles suit different types of thinkers so no individual child is at a disadvantage academically. When a particularly difficult puzzle is introduced to the group, a great feeling of camaraderie naturally develops – everyone wants to help each other to see the puzzle 'cracked'.

3. Student's problem-solving, study and social skills are improved. There is an addictive nature to puzzles which naturally captivates students and develops their concentration. While they might have developed a habit for 'giving up' through learning tasks and activities becoming too difficult or tedious, the powerful intrinsic reward of solving a puzzle helps them experience the benefits of sustained effort.

How to use puzzles in the Classroom

These activities (particularly physical puzzles) are very popular with students so they can be used as a powerful motivator. Riddles and

Mindbenders such as those below can be used as a quick fill-in activity, an early finisher task, a settling starter or as a team-building warm-up prior to a cooperative learning task.

Physical puzzles could also be used as the focus in a regular 'problem solving' session each week or as an effective relationship-building activity - 'Puzzle of the Week' – where the puzzle is made available on a 'sign-out' basis throughout the week and a record is kept ('The Puzzler's League') of those who manage to complete it. It is a good idea to buy two of each puzzle and keep a completed version of the puzzle (or a picture) on display at all times so that students know what the finished product should look like.

Wooden and metal puzzles can be bought from the following stores online:

http://www.pentangle-puzzles.co.uk

http://www.pottypuzzles.com

http://www.puzzlethis.co.uk

Here are a few Mindbenders, riddles and logic puzzles to use as quick fill-ins...

1. You are a cyclist in a cross-country race. Just before the crossing finish line you overtake the person in second place! What place did you finish in?

Second Place. If you pass the person in second, you take second place, and they become third.

2. In a year there are 12 months. 7 months have 31 days. How many months have 28 days?

They all do.

3. A plane crashes on the border of the U.S. and Canada. Where do they bury the survivors?

Survivors don't get buried.

4. I do not have any special powers, but I can predict the score of any football game before it begins. How can I do this?

Well, the score before any football game is always zero to zero!

5. You are on the bank of a river. You have to get a fox, a hen, and corn to the other site of the river. If left alone, the fox will eat the hen, the hen will also eat the corn if left alone. The boat is only big enough to take you and one other three to the other side.How do you get all 3 across intact?

First take the hen across. Leave the hen. Go back and get the fox. Take the fox to the other side. Leave the fox there, but take the hen with you back to get the corn. Leave the hen and take the corn to the other side. Drop the corn off with the fox, then go back to get the hen. Bring the hen to the other side. All 3 make it fully intact!

6. Add the following numbers in your head.

Start with 1000.

Add 40

Add 1000

Add 30

Add 1000

Add 20

Add 1000

Add 10

Write down your answer.

Many will get 5000. But the actual answer is 4100

7. What are the next 3 letters in the following sequence?
J, F, M, A, M, J, J, A, ___, ___, ___

S, O, N The sequence is first letter of the months of the year. September, October and November are the next in the sequence.

8. Jimmy's mother had 4 children. She named the first Monday. Named the second Tuesday. The third is named Wednesday. What is the name of the fourth child?

Jimmy.

9. You are driving a bus. At the first stop, 2 women get on. The second stop, 3 men get on and 1 woman gets off. Third stop, 3 kids and their mom get on, and a man gets off. The bus is grey, and it is raining outside. What colour is the bus driver's hair?

Whatever colour your hair is; you are the bus driver!

10. Before Mt. Everest was discovered, what was the highest mountain in the world?

Mt. Everest.

11. I left my campsite and hiked south for 3 miles. Turned east and hiked for 3 miles. Then turned north and hiked for 3 miles, at which time I came upon a bear inside my tent eating my food! What colour was the bear?

White. The only place you can hike 3 miles south, then east for 3 miles, then north for 3 miles and end up back at your starting point is the North Pole. There are only polar bears in the North Pole, and they are white!

12. Which came first, the chicken or the egg?

The egg. Dinosaurs laid eggs long before there were chickens!

13. A man lives on the fifteenth floor of an apartment building. Every morning he takes the elevator down to the lobby and leaves the building. In the evening, he gets into the elevator, and, if there is someone else in the elevator, he goes straight back to his floor. Otherwise, he goes to the tenth floor and walks up five flights of stairs to his apartment. Why?

The man is a dwarf. He can't reach the upper elevator buttons, but he can ask people to push them for him.

14. Crime Scene: A room has one door. The door was locked from the inside, and then nailed shut from the inside. The police break into the room. In the middle of the room there is a dead man hanging from the ceiling, his feet are 3 feet off the ground. The only other thing in the room is a hammer lying in a puddle of water and an electric fan heater. Can you explain what happened?

A creative-thinking man decided to kill himself. He got a block of ice, and put it in the middle of the room. After nailing the door shut from the inside, he switched on the fan heater, stood on the block of ice, put the noose around his neck and waited for the ice to melt. Hours later the police find him hanging with only a puddle of water, the heater and a hammer in the room.

15. Your sock drawer contains 24 white socks and 30 black socks. The lights in your room are off, so you cannot see the color of the socks. How many socks must you grab to ensure to have at least one matching pair?

Three. In the worst case, the first two socks you take out will consist of one black sock and one white sock. The next sock you take out is guaranteed to match one or the other.

16. You are in a cookie factory, and need to make a huge batch of chocolate chip cookies. The recipe calls for exactly 4 cups of sugar. Problem is that you have two buckets. One is 5 cups, the other is 3 cups. Using these buckets, can you measure exactly 4 cups of sugar? How?

Fill the 5 cup bucket. Pour it into the 3 cup bucket. This leaves 2 cups in the 5 cup bucket. Dump out the 3 cup bucket. Now pour the 2 cups from the 5 cup into the 3 cup. Refill the 5 cup. Now pour the 5 cup into the 3 cup until the 3 cup is full. That will leave exactly 4 cups in the 5 cup bucket!

17. An Arab sheik is old and must will his fortune to one of his two sons. He makes a proposition. His two sons will ride their camels in a race, and whichever camel crosses the finish line LAST will win the

fortune for its owner. During the race, the two brothers wander aimlessly for days, neither willing to cross the finish line. In desperation, they ask a wise man for advice. He tells them something; then the brothers leap onto the camels and charge toward the finish line. What did the wise man say?

"Swap Camels"

18. What can run but never walks, has a mouth but never speaks, has a head but never weeps, and has a bed but never sleeps?

A river

19. What gets wetter as it dries?

A towel

20. What is full of holes but can still hold water?

A sponge

Role-Play & Drama

John was one of the most challenging 14 year old students I've ever taught. He wouldn't listen, wouldn't sit still in his seat, was abusive and disruptive to other students and was totally negative towards any and all tasks put in front of him. He had been thrown out of mainstream school because he was unable to cope in most lessons.

One day I discovered he had a passion for acting. This normally abusive and aggressive boy, totally uninterested in normal school life, suddenly took on a whole new persona once this talent had been unearthed. He absolutely LOVED getting up in front of everyone in role plays and skits, and as long as I gave him the opportunity to do so once a week he was an entirely different boy. It was as if he needed a 'fix'. So, if you are plagued by reluctant learners perhaps some of them will benefit from role-play activities too.

For younger children role-play is a vital part of their education. It provides opportunities to play through and practice a wide range of real-life situations whilst gaining experience and practicing skills in areas such as problem solving, language and communication, numeracy, reasoning, listening etc.

For older students role-play is, again, very useful and powerful for developing social skills and also for dealing with a wide range of potentially embarrassing or sensitive social development issues such as peer pressure, drugs, bullying, race, sex, relationships etc - allowing them to explore their views and responses in a risk-free environment.

Role-play activities are exciting and above all, fun for many students and can be used to bring a dynamic element to lessons. Dull material can be brought to life and students can be given an experience which is often hard to forget.

Learning can occur during any and all of the essential elements involved in a dramatic production – from the simplest two-minute sketch right through to a full-blown mini-play complete with costumes and props. The magic moments associated with any production, from writing scripts and gathering props to directing and acting, are highly memorable for students and serve as a very powerful active learning format. Again, dull material can be transformed into a practical and enjoyable activity.

Tips for incorporating drama into lessons:

1. Avoid too much repetition

Having the whole class carry out the same role play (e.g. exploring an emotive issue such as a bullying scenario) in their respective groups at the same time is a good way to make sure all students gain experience and skills associated with taking part. However, while it is beneficial for students to watch other groups perform, it would be unfair to expect them to sit through the same play time after time. It is far better to create slight variations on a theme and change the scenario slightly for each group.

2. Engage the audience

One way of including all members of the class – even those who aren't involved in a particular performance – is to occasionally stop the play and give audience members the chance to replace one of the actors, giving an alternative course of action for the performance. This is particularly useful where there might be more than one point of view in a scenario; 'rewinding' the play and 'replaying' with a new actor who has a different agenda is an excellent way for students to fully explore an issue/topic. (Film directors lumbered with Keanu Reeves wish they could do this.)

Another way of engaging the audience is to make sure they have something specific to watch out for throughout the performance. Some students will benefit from being given a question sheet – the answers to which will be found by watching the play, while others may just need pointers such as 'make a note of all the different ways Simon offers support to his friend'.

3. Ensure students know what they are being asked to act out

Provide them with the information you have already prepared about their character(s): the goals and background information. It needs to be clear to the student how committed a character is to his/her goals and why. Outline your expectations of them as you would for any assignment, and stress what you expect them to learn in this lesson.

4. Have everyone participate

Some students will try to opt out of this activity – role-play can be quite daunting. For that reason, this is one activity in which 'friendship groups' should be encouraged.

Putting pressure on students by saying 'everyone must be involved in the acting' will turn some of them off straight away. Instead, encourage everyone to take part in the planning and those who express concern at performing can be told they can have a non-speaking part. If they later want to speak, they can do. Many students find, once they get over their initial fear, that they really enjoy role play activities and many will actively request bigger roles in the next session. One of my students who flatly refused to take part in the Christmas play eventually ended up having three parts. Once he'd got over his initial fear he found he loved getting up in front of an audience. There's no stopping him now!

5. Include a de-brief session

Like any inquiry-based exercise, role playing needs to be followed by a debriefing in which the students can define and reinforce what they have learned. This can be handled in reflective essays, or a concluding paragraph at the end of an individual written assignment, or in a class discussion. The instructor can take this opportunity to ask the students if they learned the lessons defined before the role play began.

6. Assess their efforts

Generally, grades are given for written projects associated with the role play, but presentations and even involvement in interactive exercises can be graded. Special considerations for grading in role playing exercises include:

- Playing in character - working to further the character's goals and making statements that reflect the character's perspective.

- Being constructive, courteous and showing empathy and understanding for the views of others.

8 Drama activities for the classroom

Drama activity 1: Acting content

This strategy can be used where you might normally explain a concept through teacher-talk, video or handout. Instead, the students learn by discovery – by 'experiencing' the actual idea and by actually 'becoming' the content. Virtually any concept or topic can be taught in this way with some creative thought.

Example: As a five-minute introduction to Particle Theory, the behaviour of atoms can be illustrated and experienced by putting students into groups and having them behave as particles do in the three states – solid, liquid and gas. In their solid state the students would be stood closely together in a tight group, shaking slightly or vibrating. As liquids the distance between each student would be increased and they would move around to fill a designated area. They may hold on to each other to signify occasional bonding whilst vibrating and moving more rapidly. As gases the students would move freely round the room, filling the entire space and occasionally colliding with each other. (Care needed!)

Drama activity 2: Singing content

'The Ron Clarke Story' starring Matthew Perry (from 'Friends') is an inspirational film which every teacher should watch; there are some great ideas and emotive messages throughout.

One of the ideas mentioned which you may have also used is to have students sing and dance their way through lesson content in order to make it memorable and enjoyable. The way this was done by Mr Clarke when he committed all the presidents of the USA to a rap and sang it to his class was highly amusing to watch, but when the students took the stage to do their raps the real reasons for the activity became apparent: although they had covered the same lesson content earlier and HATED it, they absolutely loved doing this activity... and they successfully learned the content.

It always surprises me how much young people love to sing – especially the reluctant learners. Being given the option of writing their own subject-based lyrics to their favourite tunes is a guaranteed winner in the classroom. You can also find ready-made lyrics and songs for a huge number of lesson topics by typing' "name of topic" song' into Google, e.g. "The Rock Cycle" song.

Drama activity 3: Mini-plays

We don't have time to produce full-blown plays complete with props and sets as described below but there are opportunities for mini-plays in every lesson. They are a powerful teaching aid and a natural active learning method – much better and more memorable than teacher-talk or videos.

Examples:

Let students take on the roles of characters in a book they are studying and allow other members of the class to question them about their background, their thoughts, their actions and their intentions.

Split the class into groups and have each group perform a short sketch (five minutes maximum) that depicts one of the events from the lesson topic. All students in each group would be involved in researching and writing scripts as well as rehearsing and performing.

Drama activity 4: Full plays

The resources, time and energy required to script and run a full-blown play in a lesson means this is a very occasional activity but it really should be considered as a possibility simply because it is such a powerful learning opportunity.

Plays for many units of study can actually be purchased in a ready-made format but in many cases it may be better to write your own. A well-written play will become one of your best teaching resources, something you can use again and again year after year to engage and delight your students.

- Plan your play well in advance. There should be sufficient parts for everyone to have at least some stage time.

- Run auditions for parts at the start of the topic/unit of study.

- Have students help source props.

- Run rehearsals as a starter to your normal lessons so that the play will be well known by the time you finish the unit of study.

- Consider adding songs to make your play a musical – kids love to sing.

- Use the play as a grand finale to your unit of study.

Drama activity 5: Assessment tools

Acting can be an incredibly effective assessment tool – certainly a nice change from the usual mini-test.

When students have learned key facts one of the best ways to get them to remember those facts or pieces of information is to have them actively involved in using the information. We covered one example of this in Review Activity 8 'Student as Teacher' ('Plenary and Review' week 3). The following example is a slightly more creative way of having students use the information they've learned in a role play activity which serves as a nice assessment method.

Example:

Students are taught the names of bones in the human skeleton. As their plenary they must take the role of surgeon and perform 'operations' on their learning partner – identifying named broken bones.

Drama activity 6: Talk show

Students are put into groups of four with one member of each group acting as the talk show host. Each 'guest' can then be invited to speak on a given topic.

Example:

This is a great way to review a book the class has been studying, with each 'guest' acting as a character in the book and giving their own story when invited by the host.

Drama activity 7: TV Program

Students love this activity and the format can be adapted to virtually any subject area. The three program types I have used with success are 'Children's TV Show', 'TV Quiz Show' and 'The News'.

Example:

Students split into groups of four or five. For 'The News' one or two students act as the main presenters, explaining key points from the lesson/subject content while another group member could act as a roving reporter to present 'breaking news' or 'on the ground' reports from key people/experts in the field.

Drama activity 8: Filming

Filming covers a wide range of learning objectives and can enhance any role play or drama session. Activity 8 above lends itself perfectly to filming and the students love watching their finished products at the end of the session. Here are some tips to get the most from filming:

- Consider filming different aspects of the plot in different locations/ rooms to give variety.

- Try and keep video sessions short and snappy. Encourage students to break their presentation up into 'scenes'.

- Encourage a question and answer session at the end of the presentation and film that too.

- As a humorous extra, allow students to include their funny 'out-takes' at the end of the show.

Magic & Illusions

I first started using magic in lessons as a result of a unit of work I was doing with my class on Shakespeare. We had been studying Macbeth and their interest in the witches led to discussions on the paranormal, which naturally led to a lesson on magic and illusions – and they enjoyed it tremendously. As a treat, I decided to show them a few simple tricks I'd learned from a friend who ran a corporate entertainment business and the response was just amazing. I couldn't believe how much interest there was in these simple tricks and illusions so I tried to show them at least one new trick each week from then on. In time students were bringing their own tricks in to show the rest of the class and it became something of a ritual to have a (excuse the pun) 'magic moment' each week.

I've split this section into two groups, 'Mind Tricks' and 'Illusions'. Students of all ages love this first form of magic in which someone apparently reads the mind of another, or foretells events yet to come. You don't need to be psychic to do these tricks-all you need to know is a few sneaky tricks.

Mind Trick 1:

Other people in school

The illusion:

Hand out three slips of paper, and ask for three student volunteers to help you. Two are to write the names of two students in the class on their slip. The third person is asked to write the name of a student from another class/year group in school.

The three slips are folded and placed in a hat, (without you touching them). You are then blindfolded, or the hat is held high over your head so that you cannot see into it. You are able to reach in and bring out the slip with name of the person in another class written on it.

How it's done:

This is a very easy trick. Take a sheet of note paper, and tear it into three pieces. The top and bottom pieces will have one smooth edge and one rough edge, but the centre piece will have two rough edges.

Make sure the person who is writing the name of the missing person writes on the centre slip while the other two students write the names of a student in their class on each of the other two slips. Have the slips folded and dropped into the hat.

When you reach into the hat, all you need to do is feel for the slip with two rough edges. When you have found it, don't bring it out right away. Have the students concentrate on the names they have written. Bring out the slip, still folded, and hold it against your head. Build up the suspense until you have created a mystery. Then reveal the slip in your hand as the one with the missing student's name. If you wish, you may leave the room while the names are being written so that all the spectator students are aware of the names that have been written, and be brought in blindfolded for a dramatic presentation.

Mind Trick 2:

Famous names

The illusion:

Have members of the audience call out the names of about ten famous people, past or present. You can adapt this trick to curriculum by having students choose key words.

Each name/word is written on a separate card. The cards are then well mixed and you make a prediction on a pad of paper as to which card you think will be picked. A student selects one of the cards. He reads his selection aloud and the name you wrote on the pad is the same as the name read.

How it's done:

You will need ten small cards or a small pad of paper to write the names on and a hat.

With everything at hand, ask someone to call out the name of a famous person/a key word associated with the lesson topic. Write this down on one of the cards and drop it into the hat. Ask for another name/word. This time do not write the name/word that is called, but write the first name/word that was called. Now both cards in the hat have the same name written on them. As different names/words are called you continue writing the original word on each card until you have about ten cards in the hat, all with the same word on them. Now write this word on the pad so that the audience does not see it.

Place the pad where it can be seen, but with the writing away from the audience. Invite a student to come up and assist you. Shake the hat to mix the cards. Ask the student to reach into the hat and select one of the cards, and read the word written on it, aloud. After he does this, turn the pad around to show that the name selected was the same as the one that you predicted on the slate. Be sure and destroy the slips after the trick, so that no one may see them.

Mind Trick 3:

The book test

The illusion:

You hand a student a sealed envelope, and display an ordinary telephone book (you can do this with a text book to relate to the curriculum). You ask the student to call out a three digit number, which you write down. Another student is asked to make certain calculations with the numbers, and announce the result. He is then asked to look in the telephone book/text book at a page indicated by the results and read a certain word on that page. The name/word in the book is the same as the word in the sealed envelope he has held all along.

How it's done:

Before you start, turn to page 108 in the telephone/text book and either count down to the 9th name on the page or count the 9th word in the first sentence. Write this name/word on a slip of paper and seal it in an envelope.

Hand the sealed envelope to a student and ask him to hold it. Ask someone else to call out a three digit number, or have three different students each call out a one digit number. Write the three digit number down in plain view, on the board or large sheet of paper.

Have another student come up to make some calculations. For example, suppose the number was 653. Ask him to reverse the number (356), and to subtract the lower number from the higher:

653-356=297

Ask him now to take the result (297), reverse it, (792) and add the two together:

297+792=1089

The answer will always be 1089, no matter what numbers are used. If only two figures result from the subtraction, be sure to add a zero at the left, such as 079.

Now ask the student with the telephone/text book to look on the page indicated by the first three numbers, 108, and to count along to the name/word indicated by the last number which is 9.

Ask him to read aloud the name that appears at that position. Have the student with the envelope open your prediction, which proves to be correct.

If you wish, you may use this as a telepathy stunt instead of a prediction stunt. In that case, do not write a prediction, but ask the spectator who is looking in the telephone/text book to concentrate on the name. With great concentration, and drama, tell him the name he is looking at. Of course you have memorized it before the start of the trick.

Mind Trick 4:

Book trick

The illusion:

You show a book, a novel, textbook, or any kind of book, and have a student insert a card anywhere he chooses. The book is opened at the page indicated by the card, and you are able to tell what is on that page, either by a written prediction, or by saying it aloud.

How it's done:

Use a book with a plain cover. Choose a page near the centre and write down the first sentence on a slip of paper or memorize it. Place a card in the book at this page.

Pick up the book, but hide the projecting card as you go to a student and hand him a plain card. Have him thrust the card into the book anywhere he wishes. Now, if you planned to use a written prediction, hand it to another student to hold. As you move about turn the book over, revealing the end from which your card projects.

If you don't use a written prediction, turn the book around as you approach another student and have him open the book to the page indicated by the card. Be sure to cover the card that still projects from the other end with your hand. As you hand the student the book, slip the card out of the book, without letting him see you do this. As the student holds the book, ask him to concentrate on the first line on the page that is indicated by the card. Then tell him what it says, or have him read it aloud and then read your prediction. Don't merely tell him that the page says so-and-so, but appear to concentrate deeply and state the sentence slowly and mysteriously.

The magic frame

The illusion:

This trick can be easily adapted to any subject area and serves as a sure-fire attention-grabber.

You show a small picture frame which contains no picture, only a black background. You cover the frame with a pocket handkerchief, then show about a dozen small cards, each bearing the name of either an object or famous face relating to the lesson subject. The cards are placed in a small bag and shaken up. A student selects one card from the bag and reads off the name of his selection. You remove the handkerchief from the frame, and it now holds a picture of the selected word/name.

How it's done:

You will need to make a small cloth bag, about 6 or 7 inches square. It is made with a cloth partition which runs the length of the bag, dividing it into two sections or compartments. These can be bought from magic shops but are very easy to make.

You will also need a picture frame with a piece of black cloth glued to the inside of the back, so that the frame has a black background when empty. Cut a piece of black cloth, the same width as the inner edge of the frame but about three inches longer, out of the same material as the background.

Now, cut a picture of a famous person, or an object, relating to the subject content, so that it will fit in the frame. Take twenty-four pieces of cardboard and print the name of this person/object on thirteen of them. On the remaining eleven cards print the names of eleven different people/objects.

Before you start the trick, place the eleven different name cards, plus one of the thirteen duplicate cards, in one side of the bag. Place the twelve duplicates in the other compartment.

Arrange the frame like this, starting from the front: first the glass, then the piece of black cloth, then the picture, and finally the background. The cloth will stick out of the top of the frame, and hang down the back.

To begin, reach into the side of the bag with the different name cards and pull them out.

Let all the students see these different cards and also show them that the frame is empty.

Place the frame, standing up, on your table and cover it with another large black pocket handkerchief or piece of cloth.

Ask a student to drop the cards into the bag (making sure they go into the empty side by holding this side open).

Shake the bag to mix the cards, then hold the bag open and ask a student to reach into it and remove one of the cards. (Make sure you only hold open the side with the duplicate cards).

Ask him to read (aloud) the name/word on the card he has selected and show it to the other students.

Pull the handkerchief/cloth off the frame, and as you do so, pull the small piece of black cloth out, hiding it in the folds of the handkerchief. You can feel the cloth through the handkerchief. Hold up the frame and show the picture. You can even take the frame apart and show that it is normal.

I'll name that vegetable in one (or maybe 'two')

This is a nice quick little starter for any lesson.

The illusion:

Tell the class you are going to give them a quick quiz and that, because you're such a great teacher, you can actually enter their minds and make sure they give you the correct answers!

You give them a series of questions, nine of which are very easy. When they write their answer to the tenth question you will show them that you already had their answer in your pocket – you forced them to be 100% A-star students!

How it's done:

Before you start, write the word 'carrot' on one side of a piece of card, and the word 'broccoli' on the other side. Stick this piece of card in your pocket.

Start by giving easy questions relating to the subject. In a maths lesson, for instance, questions might be '4 x 2', '10 + 5' etc (yes, I know, really easy – you'll probably need to make them harder but make sure they are at a level students can easily answer).

Shout out nine of these questions fairly fast – so that students have just long enough to write down the answer – and then shout out "Write the name of the first vegetable that comes into your mind".

If you see anyone 'thinking' at this point hurry them along – you don't want them to think about it!

When everyone has finished, tell students you'll now go through the answers.

Before you give the answer to question ten, tell them that you used your Jedi mind powers to 'force' them to write the name of the vegetable you wanted them to.

You can now take the piece of card that was in your pocket. Ask everyone to raise their hand if they wrote down 'carrot'.

Show them your card with carrot written on and tell them that, from now on, if they listen intently in your lessons, you can guarantee they'll get good grades.

(The most common answer is 'carrot'; generally 80-90% of students will write this name down. The second most common answer is usually 'broccoli'.)

Mind Trick 7:

"You will do as I say!"

This is a great trick to remind students that your word is final – that they really have no choice but to follow your instructions!

The illusion:

You reach into your pocket or desk drawer and start pulling out random objects – a pair of scissors, some keys, a whistle, flux capacitor, the watch from your wrist, thumb screw etc. You select three items (let's say the watch, the keys and the whistle) and place them on the desk.

"Daniel, you're going to pick one of these items and I'm going to make you pick the one I want you to pick using subliminal messaging. The key here, I'll say that again, the key here is to focus on one item and pick the one that locks (looks) right." (You make it quite obvious that you are trying to suggest the keys to Daniel by highlighting the words 'key' and 'locks'.)

Daniel smiles a smile which says "I don't think so, sir" and picks the watch.

You look surprised but then say "Well, that's very interesting Daniel, you obviously think you can ignore my instructions completely but you underestimate the power I have over you."

You point at a blank piece of paper on the desk and ask Daniel to turn it over. On the other side it reads "You will pick the watch – told you!"

How it's done:

You are actually covered no matter what object the student picks with this nifty little trick. If he picks the keys you direct him to look closely at the keys and read the key fob. On the key fob is written "Ha ha, I knew you'd pick the keys! Don't underestimate me."

By placing the keys with the fob facing down to the table, he would not see this during the trick until he picks them up.

Similarly, if he picks the whistle, you ask him to look carefully at the ribbon to which the whistle is tied. Written clearly along it are the words "Ha ha, I knew you'd pick the whistle! Don't underestimate me. " Again, he would only see these words when his attention is drawn to them – after he has picked the item.

If you happen to have a Dictaphone in your drawer a nice variation is to have a message pre-recorded... "Ha ha, I knew you'd pick the Dictaphone..."

(Note: this trick is quite adaptable, and also works with children not called Daniel.)

Mind Trick 8:

"I know what your favourite.................Is"

Another great trick – this time you are going to demonstrate your ability to read a student's mind through the science of graphology (analysing their handwriting).

The illusion:

You hand a student a pad of paper (one of those spiral notebooks will do) and tell them you're going to tell them what their favourite (*insert suitable topic here*) is by studying their handwriting. The topic could be their favourite subject in school, favourite sport, favourite holiday destination, best friend etc.

You ask them to think of their favourite..... or best friend. "I want you to write the name of this thing or person BIG on the page like this." You demonstrate by writing 'BIG' on the first page of the pad. You then tear the first page off and place it on the table.

You hand them the pad and have them write while you look away. They are then to think of four other people/places/things which they DON'T like quite as much as their favourite and write the names of these on the next four pages of the pad. They then tear off the five pages and place them on the table. They can shuffle them as much as they like while your back is turned.

You turn round and study the writing on each page and eliminate the pages one by one until their favourite is left.

"Just imagine how much I know about you every time I mark your book!"

How it's done:

The method behind this is simple and almost completely invisible. When you take the pad to write the word 'BIG' on it, turn the pad landscape style, look at the pen tip as if to check it's working and then draw a little scribble in the top left corner of the first page, pressing quite hard. Then write the word 'BIG' to fill the page, before tearing off the top page and handing the pad to the student to write their favourite item/person.

When you turn to analyse the five pieces of paper, the favourite will be the piece of paper with the most visible indentation from your test scribble. How easy is that?

Illusion 1:

Liar!

Have a pack of cards ready and note which card is on the bottom of the deck. Ask a student to select a card from the fanned-out pack. The student now shows the rest of the class the card, but not you.

While they are looking at the card, close the fan of cards and leave the pile face down on the table. Get the volunteer to cut the deck into equal piles and to place his card on the top of the pile you indicate. Now place the other pile ON TOP of the volunteer's card. The card that was at the bottom of the pack was the one YOU MEMORISED earlier and will now be on top of the volunteer's chosen card. Now ask the volunteer to say "No" every time you turn over a card, even when his/her own card has been turned up.

You say that the cards will tell you when the student is lying. You will know when the selected card is imminent because your memorised card will be the one before it. When you turn over the selected volunteer's card and your volunteer says "No", you yell out "Liar!"

Illusion 2:

Hang Ten

You need an accomplice for this trick so this is a great relationship-builder. Speak to one of your most challenging students privately before the lesson and ask if they'll help you perform a magic trick (and keep it secret). Most kids love to be involved in this sort of thing so it can be a good way to get them on side.

Select ten cards from a pack, including one Number 10 card. Place the cards upright on a table, in the same array as the spots on the Number 10 card, (H-shape).

Ask a student to select a card while you aren't looking and tell the group that your assistant will now help you figure out which card the volunteer chose.

Your assistant touches each card in turn saying "Is it this one?" Once your assistant has touched all ten cards you point to the one the volunteer chose.

You will know which card it is by the actual SPOT on the Number 10 card your assistant touched when they touched the card. It will correspond with the volunteer's choice as you have laid out your cards in the Number 10 array. This is one trick you can repeat over and over no one will be able to guess how you do it!

Illusion 3:

Card Force

Have a pack of cards ready, having memorised the top card. Tell the class you are going to select six cards from the pack at random. Take the top card (the one you have memorised) and five others from the pack.

Place the six cards in two rows of three face down, having your memorised card in the top row on the right hand (or wherever you want to place it, but remember its position!). Now here's where the force begins – ask a student to select a row. If he chooses the top row, remove the bottom three cards, if he selects the bottom row, say something like "we'll remove this row, then", making sure you keep the row with the forced card.

Get the student to now select two cards from the three remaining. Again using your patter make sure that you remove the two cards which aren't the forced one. Now you can announce that the card left is "The Ace of Spades" or whatever it is. Turn it over and reveal that you are correct!

Illusion 4:

The Disappearing Note

Hold three notes of the same value in your hand for the students to see. You will make one of them magically disappear.

Prepare a note before the trick by folding it over two thirds across. With a second note, place it over the fold, hiding the crease, but making it look like there are three in your hands. In front of the students, say that you are going to make money disappear and show the two notes (which look like three) to the students. Hold the top of the notes between your thumb and forefinger and shake them so that the folded note unfolds. The illusion of three notes becoming two is complete!

Illusion 5:

The Disappearing Coin

Put your left elbow on the table, with your hand grabbing the back of your neck. With your right hand rub a coin against your arm. Keep the coin covered so the students can't see it. Keep rubbing and then 'accidentally' drop it.

Now pick it up with your left hand and pretend to put it in your right hand. Go back to the starting position, all the while pushing the coin from your left hand into the back of your neck so it sticks there (or drops down your shirt – it doesn't matter). Show both hands to the students and the coin has magically disappeared! Be careful when you stand up.

Illusion 6:

The Hypnotised Handkerchief

You will need a drinking straw and a handkerchief that has a stitched hem big enough to fit the straw into it. Flatten the straw and thread it into one of the hems of the handkerchief.

Grasp the corner above the sewn-in straw and tie a knot in that corner, allowing the handkerchief to hang down from the knot. Tell the students you are going to hypnotise the handkerchief.

Grab the corner at the base of the straw with your other hand and release the knot end, letting it fall. Using your performance skills pretend to hypnotise the handkerchief with your free hand. Your thumb on the hand holding the handkerchief can now move the straw, causing it to slowly lift up and appear to be balanced on your fingers. Students will gasp.

Psychic Dice

You will need three dice, a tumbler full of water and a volunteer student for this trick.

Get the volunteer to drop the dice into the tumbler and ask them to hold up the tumbler then add up the numbers on the bottom of the dice. Now ask him to place the tumbler back down on the table. Reach in and grab the dice and rub them on your forehead as if to 'read the dice' with your mind and reveal the total of the dice to the volunteer.

You will know the number because you saw the dice's upper faces. You add them up in your head and subtracted that number from 21 – the answer you get is the total of the bottom faces of the dice.

Remembering that the opposite faces of a dice always add up to seven, you have three dice so three times seven is 21. If the bottom numbers were two, three and five, their total is ten. The top numbers will be five, four and two – a total of eleven. Eleven plus ten equals 21. A simple but effective trick.

Psychic Dice II

Get a student to roll three dice and then stack them one on top of the other while your back is turned. While you can't see, tell them to add up all five faces of the dice, which are hidden (that will be the two faces on the bottom and middle dice, plus the bottom face of the third die).

Now we already know that six faces in alignment will add up to 21. When you turn and see the top dice is the number three, you can quickly tell the audience that the volunteer's added number is eighteen and you'll be correct.

Illusion 9:

Psychic Clock & Die

You will need one die and a watch or clock. Ask a student to select a number from the clock but not to reveal it. Now tell them to find the opposite number on the clock (for example, three is opposite nine) and subtract the smaller number from the larger one.

To this number they must add one and remember the final number.

Roll the die and say that the number that appears on the die, plus the one on the opposite side will add up to the number they have in their head! The two faces on the die will always add up to seven (we know that already), and the math formula from the clock face will always add up to seven.

Illusion 10:

Misdirection

This one is really easy - you just have to prepare it beforehand. You will need two envelopes and two pieces of paper. First paste the two envelopes together (back to back), so you will have two pockets where you could put the papers. Then write something on one of the pieces of paper such as 'You've all got extra homework tonight' and stuff it in one of the envelopes.

Show students your blank piece of paper and let them pass it round so they can all see it really is blank. This is the misdirection. You are putting their attention on the paper that they will forget about the envelope.

After getting the paper back, fold it twice and fit it in the other pocket of the envelope.

Close the envelope and, saying your magic word, open the envelope again and remove the paper with the writing in it. Show the paper around and while doing this hide the envelope so no one will be able to inspect it.

Illusion 11:

Torn paper

Ask a student to write a word in the centre of a piece of paper and to show the other students (but not you). Ask him/her to fold the paper in half and then fold it in half again. Take the folded paper from them and rip it into small pieces, letting the pieces fall into a half-empty coffee cup on your desk.

Ask a student to stir the torn pieces of paper in the cup and as the other students watch them do this you reveal to them what the word that was written in the center of the paper.

This is really a very simple trick. By doing the trick yourself you'll be amazed how easy yet effective it is.

Get a clean sheet of paper and write your name at the centre. Try folding it once. From that point of view you know that your name is somewhere in the middle of the crease in the paper. Then try folding it in half again. You will probably notice that now your name is now in the top left portion of the twice-folded paper. Try tearing that part and you'll see that you've got your name in your hand. Of course, if you're doing the trick, you must remember not to put that part of the paper in the cup, or you will look very silly.

Whilst the students are concentrating on all the pieces being mixed into the coffee remnants, you can have a quick look at the word on the piece of paper in your hand. Very simple, but very effective (but to be safe, pick a student who doesn't know very long words).

20 Quick Ways to Bring Humour to Your Classroom

1. Tell your students to do the 'Dying z' whenever a question is too hard

I can't remember which of my favourite childhood TV programs this came from – was it 'Tiswas'? All I remember was a television studio full of people lying on their backs with their arms and legs waving in the air pretending to be dying flies. It's a great stress reliever (I still do it before going to the bank) and always causes a laugh.

2. Use theme music

A CD of TV and film theme tunes is a great investment. You can play 'Chariots of fire', 'Rocky' or 'Mission impossible' at the start of lessons, Benny Hill when you want them to change activities and 'Countdown' when you want them to answer spot questions. Just for starters.

3. Tell a funny story

It must say something about me but I have a very good stock of funny stories about mistakes I've made, embarrassing moments and accidents I've been involved in. Students LOVE to hear a funny story half way through the lesson, "Right, put your pens down, I've got another for you..." – especially when it's about their foolish teacher.

4. Put students in pairs and get them to practice reciting tongue twisters

Give them a few minutes to practice and then have a 'Twist Off' at the front of the class – the fastest tongue gets the prize.

5. Take snapshots of your students and display the photos on a notice board in your room.

Kids love to see themselves in photographs and even if the photo's aren't funny, the students will enjoy seeing them on display.

6. Encourage class comedians

It's easy to get frustrated with the class clown and the disruption they cause but if we instead see them as a positive influence we can benefit from their humour whilst giving them some help and guidance on appropriate limits and boundaries. By encouraging their humour – in the right way, perhaps by offering them fve minutes of 'cabaret time rather than constantly interrupting you – they can actually have a far better influence on the group than you probably currently believe.

7. Get a big, bright red pair of boxing gloves (or some vampire fangs, or a big inflatable hammer or a policeman's helmet etc.)

Put them on whenever the class gets too silly. (Note to teachers who see this as an appealing reward for bad behaviour: You're right; but some teachers can make this work. My favourite primary school teacher used to do this and we thought it was hilarious. He knew how to make us laugh, but he had our total respect because he also knew when and how to impose discipline. He was the model of 'firm and fair'.

8. Get a huge pair of fluffy ear muffs

Put them on whenever the class gets too noisy

9. Have a mask and snorkel

Put it on whenever the class gets too smelly. (Often a problem in my classroom in Gateshead).

10. Use sound effects

Rapturous applause when students answer questions, a machine gun when they're being cheeky etc. Technology makes this easy – most mobile phones can be plugged in to a speaker system and can be used to access all manner of sound effects.

11. Bring in your favourite stuffed toy to class

Use it as your mascot or bring it out of its box as a signal that the class is working particularly well.

12. Give students crazy gifts for answering questions correctly

E.g. Christmas cracker toys, herbal tea bags etc. The crazier the better.

13. Have a prop box and get students to give answers in the style of different characters denoted by hats or costumes

We've mentioned this before – have you got yours yet?

14. Have a 'Joke of the Day' board

Encourage students to bring in jokes of their own – offer a prize for those who read them out at the start of class.

15. Rearrange the room and get students to guess what has changed

Move the clock, the waste bin, your desk, etc.

16. Rearrange your clothing or jewelry part way through the lesson and get them to work out what has changed.

One of my lecturers used to do this and we loved it for some reason. He would go out of the room for a few seconds and then come back in having rolled up one of his sleeves, changed his tie or swapped his watch to the other wrist. It was actually a good lesson in observation because he frequently caught us out.

17. Make sure you have the weirdest 'fiddle-jar' in school

Create a box or container filled with wind-up toys, spinners, balls, bendy things, fluffy things and other things with wobbly eyes.

There's actually a serious reason for this. It will be a kid-magnet and it will make you INSTANTLY approachable outside lesson time. Young people love to look through these things and fiddle with them – and often, when they do so, they start to talk with you and relationships start to develop and deepen. And we all know that positive relationships lie at the heart of effective teaching and make classroom management much, much easier.

18. Have regular 'chill-out' sessions

School is hard work for students – they have to sit still and listen to things they're often not very interested in for six hours a day. They don't have the luxury of getting up when they want to or changing their seat. And some of those seats are really hard!

Dim the lights (or change the bulb to a green one for a super-relaxing effect), provide cushions, switch on your lava lamp, light a joss stick, pipe up the whale sounds and get everyone to lie down for ten minutes of pure relaxation. Your students will LOVE you. And guess what, they'll work harder for you too after a rest.

19. Have special dress day

Once a month – or more often if you dare, let your students come dressed up for a special theme – Weird Sock Day, Silly Hat Day, Hawaiian Shirt Day, Red Nose Day etc.

20. Set up Secret Buddies

You've heard of Secret Santa? Well this is a bit like it – all your students put their names in a bowl and each draw out the name of one of their classmates. This is their 'Secret Buddy' and it is their job to make this person happy (by sending them funny jokes, helping them etc.) without revealing their identity. Obvious rules apply – no personal attacks, no racism or toilet humour and no put downs.

Fun Fill-ins

A resource bank of fun fill-in activities can be a life-saver during those daunting times when a lesson starts to go wrong. At times like this, to avoid classroom chaos, you need to quickly change the tone of the lesson, grab every student's attention and collect your thoughts. Fill-ins are also a great way to infuse a lesson with positive emotions and cement teacher/student relationships.

Fun Fill-In Activity 1:

'I am the Captain of the Ship'

Overview: A game to **develop listening skills** and settle a group who have lost interest with an activity or become too boisterous.

Number of people: Unlimited

Age: Any

Materials: None

Time: 5 – 15 minutes

Directions:

1. Have everyone sit quietly and say:

"I am the captain of the ship. I'm packing some carrots. What would you like to pack?"

(Only items that begin with the first letter of the speaker's name – e.g. Captain/Carrots - can be packed but this fact is not explained to the students – they have to work it out).

2. Invite students, one at a time, to suggest another object to pack for the journey.

For example, the first student might say...

"My name is John and I'm packing some shorts."

To which you would reply...

"Oh I'm so sorry John. I'm afraid you can't take your Shorts, but you could take a Jumper if you wanted to."

(Extra emphasis can be given to the first letter as the game progresses.)

3. Continue inviting students to offer an object to add to the 'packed items' list.

When a student guesses the pattern tell them not to tell other students what it is. Instead, have them keep playing the game, adding more items to the list. At first it may be difficult to get the group to settle into this activity but gradually the intrigue will build up and they will all want to take part and find the secret to taking their items on board the ship. If you have problems getting them quiet to start the activity write the opening statement on the board rather than saying it out loud.

Notes/Variations:

1. Pick words which have double consonants: hammer, bottle, pebble etc.

2. Include an accompanying code or gesture, eg:

- Innocently say "Ok..." every time it's your turn to speak prior to the actual sentence. ("Ok... I am the Captain of the ship and I'm..."). Only students who realise that they have to add the "Ok" will be able to take their items.

- Subtly scratch your nose or ear as you say your sentence.

Students will have to pay extra attention to spot these little nuances.

Fun Fill-In Activity 2:

'Pay Attention'

Overview: A quick activity to mark a transition time, re-focus a listless group and remind students how easy it is not to notice things around us unless we are paying attention.

Number of people: Unlimited

Age: Any

Materials: None

Time: 5 minutes

Directions:

1. Quickly change three or four things about your appearance without the students noticing, eg take your tie off (if you're wearing one), put your wrist watch on the opposite wrist, take earrings out, brush hair to side, roll sleeves up etc.). Tell them that you have just made some changes. Can they guess what they are?

2. After they guess, put students into pairs telling each one who is A and who is B.

3. Invite the Bs to close their eyes and count to ten slowly and all together.

4. While B's eyes are closed, A should change something about his/her appearance.

5. On the count of 10, B can open his/her eyes and try to identify the difference.

6. Then give B the chance to adjust something and let A guess. If there is time, allow students to change partners and do it again.

Skill Test 1 – Following written instructions

Overview:

This activity teaches the importance of following written instructions in a non-judgmental, entertaining way. Students complete a 'mock test' and almost always score ZERO – purely because they didn't read the instructions correctly before starting.

Provide students with a small sheet of writing paper. Then let them know that the activity you are about to do will prove how well they listen and follow directions. Let them know that you will state each instruction, then pause, then repeat the instruction. Add, I will not repeat any instruction a third time, so you must listen very carefully. Proceed to give students the instructions below.

Number of People: Any group size split into sub-groups of 6-10

Time: 5 minutes

Materials: One copy of the 'Skills Test 1' for each student.

Directions:

1. Introduce the activity by saying that it is a special test which will assess how well they follow written instructions.

2. Have students sit in 'test conditions' with desks moved apart from each other and insist on no talking or copying.

3. Hand out the papers face down and tell students they will only have 15 minutes to complete the test so they will have to work quickly. (In reality they will only need a couple of minutes but telling them they have more time normally ensures they rush through and make the desired mistakes).

4. Instruct them to turn their papers over and begin.

5. Be prepared for groans after five minutes or so – as students realise they made a crucial mistake by not reading ALL the questions BEFORE they began the test.

6. Discuss with students how they feel having made the mistake and what they can learn from the exercise.

Fun Fill-In Activity 4:

Skill Test 2 – Following verbal instructions

Overview:

This activity develops listening skills and teaches the importance of following verbal instructions in a non-judgmental, entertaining way. Students complete a very simple 'listening test' and almost always find themselves having difficulty because they don't listen attentively.

This activity can be repeated (using different instructions) and graded throughout the term to give students feedback on their improved listening skills.

Provide students with a small sheet of writing paper. Then let them know that the activity you are about to do will prove how well they listen and follow directions. Let them know that you will state each instruction, then pause, then repeat the instruction. Add, But I will not repeat any instruction a third time, so you must listen very carefully. Proceed to give students the instructions below.

Number of People: Any group size – students work individually.

Time: 5 minutes

Materials: A set of suitable questions such as those below. Lined paper and pencil for each student.

Directions:

1. Provide each student with a piece of lined paper and a pencil.

2. Explain that the following activity will assess how well they listen to people.

3. Tell them you will give them an instruction which they must follow and that you will repeat the instruction ONCE only. They must listen very carefully.

4. Sample instructions are as follows (These will need to be modified depending on the age group):

    (1) Put your surname and first initial on the third line up from the bottom of your paper.

    (2) Fold your paper in half down the longest side then open the paper out and turn it over so that the fold is sticking up.

    (3) Write the number 'one' at the top of the paper on the fold.

    (4) Fold the paper in half the opposite way, along the short edge.

    (5) Open the paper out and put a dot in the middle of the paper where the two folds cross.

    (6) Poke your pencil through the middle of the paper to make a small hole where the two folds cross.

    (7) Draw a square around the hole with sides approximately 3cm long.

    (8) Write your name on the first line of your paper in the left hand corner.

    (9) On the horizontal fold, write the numbers one to six so that there are three numbers on either side of the vertical fold.

    (10) Put a circle around the first number to the right of the hole you made in the paper.

Fun Fill-in Activity 5:

Crazy Lists

Overview:

Creating lists is a great way to develop thinking skills and when you make the lists a little crazy you add a little humour to the classroom too. As a quick fill-in, settling starter or relationship-building activity, this is a winner.

Number of People: Any group size – students work in pairs.

Time: 5-10 minutes

Materials: Paper/pens and a copy of the List Headings for each Learning Pair.

Directions:

1. Divide the group into learning pairs and issue the materials.

2. Each pair is to pick two headings from the list and produce a 'Top Ten' under each heading.

Variation:

Stick three copies of each List Heading on the board on separate pieces of card. Have one person from each learning pair come up to the board and select ONE heading to work on. When the learning pair have completed their first list they can then go back to the board to get a second heading.

List headings:

Crimes committed by Santa Claus

Things Homer Simpson would never do

Meals you would never find in a posh restaurant

Causes of broken biscuits

Things you can't buy

Flavours of crisp you can't buy

Interesting words beginning with 'J'

What you shouldn't wear at the beach

Things you would miss if you were stuck on a desert island

Alternative words for 'money'

Ways to say 'Thank you'

Ways to show you're sorry

Cartoon baddies

Ways to eat a Cream Egg

Ways to get rich

Things you could train a worm to do

Things I would need on a trip to the moon

Things I would need on a fishing trip

Scary films

Fun Fill-in Activity 6:

Charades

Overview:

This is an enjoyable way to develop students' speaking and presenting skills as well as being an effective means to cement relationships and build class community.

Number of People: 5-30

Time: Depends on group size – allow 10-15 minutes for a small group.

Materials: A list of age-appropriate film and book titles. (You can get each student to write down ten book and film titles and put them in a hat to give a wide selection).

Directions:

1. Divide the group into two teams

2. A volunteer from one team takes a card from the hat with either a book or film title written on it and has to mime the title to his/her team.

3. The team has two minutes to guess the title. If they guess within one minute they get two points, if they guess within two minutes they get one point. The guess is passed to the other team for a bonus point if they fail to guess the correct answer.

4. Teams swap over and a volunteer from the other team takes a turn at miming a new title.

Interesting Power Points

There are some amazing pictures on the internet and they can easily be pasted onto slides and shown as a quick presentation to fill a couple of minutes, settle a group, stimulate discussion, practice presentation skills or introduce a new activity. There are some ready-made presentations in the online resource area here:

http://needsfocusedteaching.com/kindle/fun/

Category Battleships

Overview: Peer relationships are developed in this fun activity in which students work together to guess items in categories.

Number of people: Any.

Materials: Two lists of categories, e.g. things that are dry/wet/hot/cold; things you can eat/drink/wear/sit on; things you can see at the park/seaside/cinema/concert; things made of wood/plastic/metal/glass; things that fly/swim/grow/move very fast etc. Obviously this activity can be adapted to most curriculum subjects by choosing appropriate categories..

Time: 10 minutes.

Directions:

1. Put the class into two teams and give each team a different list of four or five categories, eg:

i. Things found in the kitchen

ii. Animals found in a zoo

iii. Items of clothing

iv. Sports equipment

2. Each team writes down five items for each category.

3. Teams take it in turns to try to guess the items the other team has written: a member from Team One reads out one of their category titles, and then Team Two have one minute to try and guess as many items from Team One's list of five items as possible.

For every correct guess, Team Two will receive one point. At the end of the minute, Team One will receive one point for each item that hasn't been guessed.

4. Teams swap over – Team One tries to guess the items in one of Team Two's categories.

Example:

One of Team One's categories is 'Animals found in a zoo' and they choose 'giraffe', 'monkey', 'zebra', 'rhinoceros' and 'lion'.

After one minute Team Two guess 'lion', 'monkey', 'giraffe' and 'zebra'. They don't manage to guess 'rhinoceros' so they get four points and Team One gets one point.

Fun Fill-in Activity 9:

Scattergories

Number of people: Any.

Materials: A list of categories such as those above.

Time: 10 minutes.

Overview: Peer relationships and social skills are developed in this activity in which students work in pairs or in groups to create lists of unique words with the same initial letter in categories. This game is taken from the popular board game of the same name. Can be adapted to any curriculum subject.

Directions:

1. Divide the class into two teams.

2. Write four or five broad categories on the board such as: 'Countries', 'Films', 'Foods', 'Jobs', 'Buildings'.

3. Ask a student to call out a letter (excluding 'x', 'q' and 'z').

4. Start a timer and give students/groups three minutes to try and think of one word for each category. Students write down one word for each category title.

5. After three minutes players/teams read out/reveal their answers and score a point – but only if other teams don't have their word.

6. After each round the initial letter is changed.

Fun Fill-in Activity 10:

Pictionary

Overview: Peer relationships and social skills are developed in this activity in which students work in pairs or in groups to guess words from pictures. This game is adapted from the board game of the same name. Can be adapted to any curriculum subject.

Number of people: Any.

Materials: Scraps of paper for students to write on. Drawing implements.

Time: 10 minutes.

Directions:

1. Split the class into two teams.

2. Members of each team thinks of words for the other team to guess and writes them on slips of paper.

3. A player from Team One is given a word from Team Two. He/she then has to draw a picture to represent the word on the board for his team mates to guess the word. The artist is not allowed to speak.

4. If the team guesses the word within one minute they get 2 points. If they guess within 2 minutes they get one point.

5. Teams swap – a member from Team Two is given a word to draw from Team One.

Fun Fill-in Activity 11:

Spot the Difference

Overview: Peer relationships and social skills are developed in this activity in which students work in pairs or in groups to find the differences between two pictures. This activity can be used as a fill-in or as a topic-related starter depending on the pictures used and can therefore be adapted to any curriculum subject.

Number of people: Any

Materials: Search the internet for free spot the difference printable resources.

Time: 10 minutes.

Directions:

1. Split the class into teams or pairs.

2. Two slides consisting of 'almost' identical pictures are put on display.

3. Teams/pairs have a set time in which to find all the differences between the two pictures.

4. The wining team is the first to find all the differences.

But first you've got to find them!

Crazy Questions

Overview:

A simple but creative fill-in which gets students doing exactly what we spend hours trying to make them do... THINK! Don't regard this as just a pointless way to fill in some time - Crazy Questions can actually be an incredibly useful and powerful way to build bonds with students and create cohesion within a group. There's no better way to build bonds than to 'chew the cud' together and Crazy Questions are guaranteed to be the stimulus to get your students talking.

Number of people: Any.

Materials: A number of weird and wonderful, thought-provoking questions to which there are no right or wrong answers (see below for some ideas).

Time: 10 minutes.

Directions:

1. Provide a pile of 'Crazy Question Cards' – one big pile, face down in a central location such as on your desk.

2. Students work in pairs and one person from each pair picks a card blind from the pile. Students debate the interesting and stimulating questions in their pairs and then share their ideas as a group.

Variation:

Run the session as a cozy 'circle time' activity.

Sample questions to get you started:

How would you explain the colour of the wind to a blind person?

What's better – good looks or brains?

Is the best way to deal with criminals to put them in prison?

What is the meaning of life? Why are we here?

Can you choose not to love someone?

Would you rather be rich and unhealthy or poor and healthy?

What do people think of you?

If I stop looking at someone do they still exist?

If a fairy appeared and said she could put a spell on you which meant you would never make a mistake again would you let her do it?

Am I the same person I was two years ago? 6 months ago? 1 week ago? Yesterday? A minute ago? A second ago?

If I'm different to the person I was when I was a baby/yesterday, is a photo of me as a baby/yesterday really a photo of me?

Is it ever acceptable to tell a lie?

What was man's greatest invention?

Do I weigh less if I breathe out and then hold my breath?

Do things tend to work out for the best? Do things always go wrong? If so, what's the point of trying?

When is your birthday if you were born at midnight?

What would happen if... (this is a great start to a rabbit warren of debatable possibilities)

- we ran out of oil overnight?

- your mum won the lottery?

- we found a cure for all disease?

Caption Competition

Overview:

Peer relationships and social skills are developed in this activity in which students work in pairs or in groups to add speech bubbles, thought bubbles or silly titles to a variety of pictures. Students love to take part in this – it's a real mood lifter - and the finished results can be a good way to bring humour to a tired area of wall space.

Number of people: Any.

Materials: A variety of funny pictures, easily obtainable from the billions on the web.

Time: 10 minutes.

Directions:

1. Source suitable images from the net, newspapers or magazines. Doing a search for 'funny captions' using Google's 'image search' facility threw up the one above together with 660,000 others. Captions can easily be removed using image software such as 'Snagit'.

2. Put the image up on the board/wall and give students five minutes to work in pairs or groups to come up with the best caption and then share as a group.

Fun Fill-in Activity 14:

Paper Aeroplanes

Overview:

A delightful way to take the boredom out of question/answer sessions and keep students on task.

Number of people: Any.

Materials: Several pre-made paper planes. When opened, each plane should have a question relevant to the lesson topic written on it. For some excellent design variations – with video instructions! – visit:

http://www.paperairplanes.co.uk/planes.php

Time: A few seconds now and again throughout the lesson.

Directions:

Simply launch a plane in the direction of your eager audience. Whoever catches the plane opens it, reads the question and answers it.

I know what you're thinking - once students have cottoned on to the fact that they will have to answer a question if they catch the plane, they will sit like stuffed lemons whenever it comes within grabbing distance. To get round that you either have to fit a homing device or, more practically, offer more incentive to get them involved such as the chance to relaunch the plane in your direction once they've answered the question. Still not enough to interest them? Tell them if they can get it in your mouth they get the rest of the lesson off!

Variation:

As an off-topic lesson break, a five minute 'paper plane building & flying' session is a great stress reliever and can change the mood of any downbeat group. Give students a minute or two to build their planes and then draw a big target on the board for them to aim at. Closest to the bulls eye wins a speedboat.

Fun Fill-in Activity 15:

Dance Off

Overview:

A brilliant, if not essential, way to add hilarity to ALL your lessons whilst injecting learning-boosting oxygen to your students' bodies.

Number of people: Any.

Materials: A CD or MP3 full of top disco tunes – the type guaranteed to get you on your feet and shaking your booty... um... daddio.

Time: A few seconds now and again throughout the lesson.

Directions:

1. Students work in table groups.

2. Explain that you will be playing a tune at various points throughout the lesson. Let them hear a sample of the tune so they know what's coming. It should be sufficiently 'cheesy' – anything from Saturday Night Fever will do. Tell them that as soon as they hear the tune they must get on their feet and strut their stuff, throwing out the best moves they can muster.

3. Allocate points quickly at the end of each 'Dance Off' – only giving points to table groups in which all members of the team are on their feet.

4. Keep a record of points and award prize at the end of the week to the winning team such as an early finish, less homework etc.

5. Yes, I do have a suit like that.

Stand-Up

Overview:

Do you have any students in your class who are desperate for attention and always vying for the title of class clown? Of course you do, we all do. Here's a creative way of dealing with them which gives them the attention they need whilst giving you, and everyone else in the room, a good chuckle.

Number of people: Any.

Materials: A funny student skilled in the art of Stand-Up Comedy.

Time: A few minutes at the beginning, middle or end of the lesson.

Directions:

1. Speak to the student/s outside class and tell them that while their humour is tremendous, it gets to be a pain when they disrupt people who are trying to work. You have a solution – you'll give them a designated time and place to entertain everyone as long as they agree not to disrupt the rest of the lesson.

If you have a particularly talented comedian in your hands you could ask them to theme their material on the topic of the lesson. You could designate a corner of the room as 'the stage', drape a red velvet curtain on the wall, give them a mock microphone and a stool and change your classroom to The Comedy Club.

Who knows, this could become a regular slot in your lessons and you might even be able to start charging an entry fee.

And here's a quick joke for you in case you get asked to do a turn...

A professor stands up before his philosophy class and picks up an empty mayonnaise jar. He then proceeds to fill it with golf balls and asks the students if the jar is full. They agree that it is. He then picks up a box of small pebbles and pours them in the jar. He shakes it and the pebbles roll into the areas between the golf balls. He then asks the students if they think the jar is full. They agree that it is. The professor next picks up a bag of sand and pours some into the jar. Once more he asks the students if the jar is full and they agree that it is. Finally he picks up two cans of beer, opens them and pours them into the jar. "Now", says the professor. "I want you to recognize that this jar represents your life. The golf balls are the important things – your family, your children, your health and your friends. If everything else were lost and only they remained, your life would still be full. The pebbles represent your job and the important things you buy with your earnings such as your house. The sand represents the small stuff - your possessions, your hobbies etc. If you put the sand into the jar first, there's no room for the other, more important things – the pebbles and the golf balls. But remember, no matter how full your life may seem, there's always room for a couple of beers!!*

Or, if you don't have as much time, a really quick one:

News just in – a dwarf psychic has robbed a bank. Police have announced a small medium at large.

Fun Fill-in Activity 17:

Fun Dominoes

Overview:

This is a fun way to test students' ability to listen and follow written instructions.

Number of People: Any

Time: 10 minutes

Materials: A set of **Fun Domino Cards** with appropriate written instructions on them can be found in the online resource area here:

http://needsfocusedteaching.com/kindle/fun/

Directions:

1. Give each student a Domino Card with a written instruction on it.

2. The instruction on each card will be in the following format:

"After somebody_____, then you must_____"

The instruction on one card will lead to another card and so on. (card one – the starting card - will be slightly different and will simply have one instruction).

E.g.

Card 1:

"Stand up and shout "I'm sooooo happy!"

Card 2:

"After somebody stands and shouts "I'm soooo happy!", then you must stand up and clap your hands five times."

Card 3:

"After somebody stands up and claps five times, then you must do five star jumps and then shout 'That was five star jumps!'"

Etc.

3. The game continues until all students have completed their tasks. The exercise can then be repeated to see if they can improve their time.

Fun Fill-in Activity 18:

Deep Relaxation

Overview:

This may be in the 'fun' section but relaxation is a very important skill to learn and a tremendous aid to learning. With some groups, at certain times of the day (year nine straight after PE for example), having a brief period of relaxation at the start of the lesson is a necessity and once your students get used to this (and get over the initial silliness that any new and slightly different activity brings), they will really look forward to it and will welcome the chance to really 'chill out' and have a break from the constant pressures of noise and visual stimuli.

The benefits of relaxation are many, and it's worthwhile taking the time to outline these to pique student interest. People who develop their ability to relax at will claim, among others:

- heightened creativity

- clarity of thought

- the ability to calm down and settle nerves (of supreme importance at exam time)

- development of a generally more alert mind (helpful, for instance, during sports)

This exercise however carries a warning - it's so powerful that some of your students might actually nod off. Of course you might, depending on who succumbs, decide it's better not to wake them.

These easy to learn techniques reduce stress and anxiety, relax you, improve your sleep and develop a growing sense of inner calm and control that flows over into all areas of your life. The effects are immediately noticeable, but you must practise daily for a couple of months to achieve maximum benefits.

Number of people: Any.

Materials: N/A

Time: A few minutes at the beginning, middle or end of the lesson.

Directions:

There are many ways to achieve a deeply relaxed physical and mental state. You'll find one of them free in any bottle of wine but we think the two methods below are more suited to school use (and cheaper). In all seriousness, the methods do work, and they work very well, but it is definitely a good idea to start with just a few minutes at first. As with most things, you get better with practice.

Method one: Focus on the breath

You'll find a similar method to this used in some meditation classes. It is an excellent and very simple way to clear the mind and slow the brain waves down towards the relaxing 'alpha' state.

1. Sit upright in a comfortable position. Sitting comfortably on most school furniture is a feat in itself but try to send some time on this first step as it is important. Encourage students to sit upright, as though there is a piece of string pulling them upwards from the top of their heads.

2. Once they are sitting correctly and comfortably, the next step is to practise a little 'high quality breathing' using the diaphragm and entire thoracic cavity.

Step One

This step uses the diaphragm to fill the lower part of the lungs. Breathe in so that your stomach expands but your chest stays still. Exhale with the chest still and the stomach falling. If you put your hand on your belly you should feel it rise and fall with each breath. Repeat for 10 breaths.

Step Two

This step uses the muscles in between the ribs to expand the chest cavity and fill the top portion of the lungs. This time breathe in so that your chest rises, while your stomach is still. Exhale so that your chest goes down again, while your stomach remains still. Repeat for 10 breaths.

Step three

Now that you've mastered these first two stages, step three brings them both together into one breath.

Begin by stomach breathing. When you feel you can't inhale any more in this manner, switch to chest breathing, until the upper part of your lungs are filled. Then exhale by chest breathing first, progressing to stomach breathing so that you empty the lungs fully. Continue breathing like this for 5 minutes.

Once steps one and two are learned, step three is the exercise that you can use any time for a few minutes to calm the nervous system or, as we'll use it here, to prepare for some deeper relaxation.

The next step is to calm the body by focusing concentration on the breath leaving and entering the body. During this stage students continue to sit upright but are encouraged to now breath normally - instead of trying to breathe deeply, they just 'breathe'. My meditation teacher summed up the process perfectly in once sentence: *'Take it easy, take it as it comes, do less and accomplish more.'*

The idea is simply to sit with eyes closed and 'watch' (using the mind's eye) the breath entering and leaving the belly. Note that the emphasis is on breathing normally i.e. not to try to breathe fast/slow/deep/shallow – just to breathe normally and put attention on the belly area.

Method two: Focus on the body

To take it seriously, students need to be told how beneficial deep relaxation is. Deep relaxation is very easy to learn and only requires 10 minutes' practice twice each day but the benefits to health are amazing. Every time you carry out these exercises you will teach your body how to relax – something that it has no doubt forgotten in this busy world of ours!

I use the following script which is common to many self-hypnosis type programs and meditation courses. There are literally hundreds and they all follow more or less the same format. If you read through the following instructions though you'll see that there's nothing complicated, it's just a case of focusing on each body part in turn, putting your awareness on that area and feeling it relax.

The exercise ca actually be done in a sitting or standing position as well as lying down flat. Lying down might not be possible in some classrooms without mats of some sort – better to go through the instructions with students in a sitting position.

Here's the script:

'Rest comfortably looking straight ahead. Don't stare hard but 'gaze' at one spot. Close your eyes if it becomes an effort to keep them open but don't try and force anything – just relax, let go.

The object of this resting is to quietly and gently let your mind and body gradually slow down of their own accord. You can't force this. Just let go.

If your mind starts racing off, working out problems or thinking of things you have to do just gently bring your attention to the spot on the ceiling. And let go. And when your eyes become too heavy to keep open, let them close.

After a short while you will start to become aware of tiredness throughout your body of which you were not conscious before. You will start to feel these sensations of tiredness specifically located in various muscles in the arms, legs, back, shoulders and feet. The body is letting go.

Close your eyes and feel these sensations in your body.

Now direct your attention to your feet. Feel your feet with your mind. Feel the soles of the feet, the toes and the tops of the feet. Feel your feet relax. Feel the skin relax. Feel the bones relax. Feel the cells relax.

You will probably feel some sort of tingling sensation in your feet as you think about them. This is ok, your feet are relaxing.

Now move your attention to your calves and shins. Feel your calves and shins relax. Feel the skin relax. Feel the bones relax. Feel the muscles relax. Feel the cells relax.

You will probably feel some sort of tingling sensation in your calves and shins as you think about them. This is ok, your calves and shins are relaxing.'

After a brief pause continue the script, moving up through the various parts of the body – thighs, stomach, back, shoulders, arms/hands, neck, head, face – lips, mouth, tongue etc.

Once you have gone through the whole sequence ask students to tense all their muscles - from curling their toes right up to screwing up their faces - and hold for a few seconds. Repeat this and then get them to relax again deeply with their eyes closed. They should now be very relaxed if they have followed all the instructions. Some, of course, may be asleep!

Let them lie quietly for five minutes or so before resuming the lesson. When they are in this deeply relaxed state you could also play some chilled out music or ask them to visualize a goal that they want to achieve. Most young people love to use this type of imagery.

Energisers

Energisers are generally quick activities designed to stimulate thinking, raise flagging energy levels or to spark motivation in an activity. They can be used at the beginning of a group session or class, as well as in the middle or at the end. They are also a wonderful way to build group cohesion and stimulate interaction because they depend on the group's cooperation, participation, and interest to complete the activity.

Please don't make the mistake of discounting energisers as a waste of time. You will waste far more time by having to deal with students who are bored, listless, lacking in energy and in need of an activity change. Energisers, when used appropriately, can maintain the attention of an otherwise troublesome class.

They also have the added bonus of helping boost memory. Physical activity – even in very short bursts - increases production of the memory fixatives norepinephrine and epinephrine, and triggers the release of glucose (which also supports memory functions) from glycogen stores in the liver.

Where possible, we try to include activities which will suit both a 'normal' class size (25-40 students) as well as smaller nurture/special groups (2-8 students). For a guideline as to the suitability for different group sizes refer to the 'Number of people' heading in the activity intro.

Please note:

It can be useful to outline the purpose of each activity to your students (as stated in the activity introduction) and to ask them a few processing questions at the end.

Questions such as 'How did you feel about that?', 'Did the activity help you feel more comfortable with the group/relax/warm up/have fun?', 'What did you get out of that exercise?' or did you feel uncomfortable in any way?' help participants see the activities as a learning experience as opposed to just 'game playing' although too much emphasis on these questions can frustrate students and make them feel very negative about what they previously felt to be an enjoyable experience. Use with caution and be sensitive to their reactions.

Finally, it may be helpful to bear in mind the following points when selecting an activity:

- Time of day and weather (younger children in particular are affected by extreme weather and may become over-excited with some of the activities).

- Room restrictions. 'Health and Safety'

- The way participants are dressed.

- 'Mood' of the group or individuals within the group.

- Special Educational Needs of students

Energiser 1:

'Write Your Name'

Number of people: Unlimited

Materials: None

Time: 5 minutes

Purpose: To re-focus a group. To provide some light relief following intense working period. To raise energy levels.

Directions:

The group stands in front of the leader. The leader instructs the group to take their right hands and write their first names in the air with an imaginary pen/pencil.

Next, they are asked to write their last names in the air with their left hands. (Usually that's more difficult.)

Next they have to write their first and last names; but... they have to put their hands behind their backs and pretend they have a pen/pencil in their mouths to write their names.* Remember to dot every "i" and cross every "t".

* Explain that they must write 's-l-o-w-l-y' and make them aware of the danger of sharp head movements. (Health and Safety, remember!)

Alternatives to 'pen in the mouth':

Place pen in ear, in elbow, in belly button, on end of shoe, in the middle of back etc.

NB// pen in the belly button always gets a laugh but be prepared for vulgar gestures from older students.

Energiser 2:

'Footsteps'

Number of people: Unlimited

Materials: None – although open space required by moving chairs/ tables to side of room.

Time: 5 minutes

Purpose: To re-focus a group. To provide some light relief following intense working period. To raise energy levels.

Directions:

Ask everyone to stand up and find a space to move around in. Explain that they will perform actions to demonstrate different types of shoes:

Walking boots	(Walk)
Ballet shoes	(Dance)
Trainers	(Press ups)

Wellington Boots	(Simulate muddy terrain by raising knees high)
High Heels	(Walking daintily on tip toes)
*Sandals	(Lie down and sun bathe)
Riding boots	(Trot round as if on a horse)
Dress Shoes	(Walk gracefully, head held high, greeting each other politely)

Call out the names of the shoes in any order and ask class members to make the appropriate actions.

After a short while end with 'Sandals' or 'Slippers' and allow time to relax before moving into the next activity.

Alternatives:

* If floor is dirty, substitute 'Slippers' (Sit down relaxing).

Energiser 3:

'Zip, Zap, BOING!'

Number of people: Unlimited

Materials: None

Time: 5-10 minutes

Purpose: To re-focus a group. To provide some light relief following intense working period. To raise energy levels.

Directions:

Have everyone stand in a circle facing each other. One person starts off by saying 'ZIP' and mimes throwing a ball or frisbee dramatically at the person on their left. (The 'throwing' can be as dramatic as possible – as demonstrated by the leader).

This message (ZIP) and the same action is passed on around the circle from person to person – one person mimes throwing and saying "ZIP" while the next person mimes catching before passing on.

After one whole round introduce the next word... "ZAP". When a person is passed the Frisbee or ball they now have the choice of putting their hands in the air and saying "ZAP". When they do this, the ball/ Frisbee bounces off them and goes back to the person who threw it. This person must now start throwing it in the opposite direction to the person on their right.

Finally you can introduce "BOING". When a person is passed the object they can now jump in the air whilst pointing across the circle at a person of their choice shouting "BOING" and the object is passed to this new person who then decides to "ZIP", "ZAP" or "BOING".

(Thanks to The People's Theatre in Newcastle for that one.)

Energiser 4:

'Film Quotes'

Number of people: Unlimited

Materials: None, but take care with Eddie Murphy films

Time: 5-10 minutes

Purpose: To re-focus a group. To provide some light relief following intense working period. To raise energy levels.

Directions:

1. Write on the board or say "Which film is this from?"

2. Write or say a quote from a famous film and invite students to guess the film. Here are a few to start you off...

"I'll be back."

(The Terminator)

"My Mama always said, 'Life was like a box of chocolates; you never know what you're gonna get.'"

(Forrest Gump)

"Adrian!!"

(Rocky)

"A census taker once tried to test me. I ate his liver with some fava beans and a nice chianti."

(The Silence of the Lambs)

"My preciousssss"

(The Lord of the Rings: The Two Towers)

"I'm (the) king of the world!"

(Titanic)

Tip:

Get students to spend a few minutes writing down quotations from films on separate pieces of paper. Put the slips of paper in a hat so that you have a supply of quotes to choose from.

Energiser 5:

'Colour Mix-up'

Number of people: Unlimited

Materials: Coloured A4 pieces of paper – Blue, Red, Pink, Yellow, Orange, Green

Time: 3-5 minutes

Purpose: To re-focus a group. To provide some light relief following intense working period. To raise energy levels. To stimulate left brain/ right brain thinking.

Directions:

1. Take 10-20 coloured pieces of paper and write a colour on each piece (different to the colour of the paper) eg:

2. Tell students they have to shout out the WORD on each paper as you hold them up in turn.

3. You can speed up to make it more challenging.

Adaptations/Variations:

This activity works very well on an interactive whiteboard when produced as a Powerpoint presentation – there is one waiting in the online resource area here:

http://needsfocusedteaching.com/kindle/fun/

Singing in a Round

Number of people: Unlimited

Materials: None

Time: 3-5 minutes

Purpose: To re-focus a group. To provide some light relief following intense working period. To raise energy levels. To build group cohesion.

Directions:

1. Section off participants into groups or rows.

2. Start one group off singing a familiar song such as 'row, row, row your boat' or 'London's Burning'.

3. Start another group when the previous group has reached the end of the first phrase in the song.

4. Continue adding other groups to the round.

Energiser 7:

Slow Breathing

Number of people: Unlimited

Age group: Any

Materials: None.

Time: 10 minutes

Purpose: To re-focus a group. To provide some light relief following intense working period. To raise energy levels. To settle nerves and build confidence.

Directions:

1. Invite everyone to take ten slow, calming breaths. Some groups get silly at this point so you might have to give them a little background as to why they are being asked to do this. Tell them this is an advanced yoga technique used by highly advanced spiritual gurus living in caves in the Himalayas and that it will give them mental clarity, poise and may possibly develop their sixth sense and psychic capabilities. That is often sufficient to arouse their curiosity and get them to try the activity. You might also give them more detailed, specific instructions so that they have less apparent freedom to mess around.

2. Take a slow breath in for the count of four, hold the breath for a count of twelve before breathing out slowly for a count of eight. This breathing cycle in the ratio of 1:3:2 is actually very calming.

Energiser 8:

'Mirrors'

Number of people: Unlimited

Age group: Any

Materials: None.

Time: 5 minutes

Purpose: To re-focus a group. To provide some light relief following intense working period. To raise energy levels. To stimulate left brain/ right brain thinking. To revitalize tired muscles.

Directions:

1. Put students in pairs – identified as 'A's and 'B's.

2. Have 'Student A' do hand or stretching motions while 'Student B's simultaneously imitates or 'mirrors' the partner's motions.

3. Invite partners to switch roles and/or switch partners.

Energiser 9:

'Touch Blue'

Number of people: Unlimited

Age group: Any

Materials: None

Time: 5 minutes

Purpose: To re-focus a group. To provide some light relief following intense working period. To raise energy levels.

Directions:

1. Call out the name of a colour and have students scurry to touch any object of that colour or any person wearing a garment of the colour.

2. Identify other objects/materials/distinctions such as 'something glass', 'something wooden', 'something plastic', 'something round', 'something hollow' etc.

Fun Energiser 10:

Horseplay

Number of people: Groups up to 40 maximum.

Materials: Imaginary horses, as long as they aren't too frisky.

Time: 5 minutes.

Purpose: To re-focus a group. To provide some light relief following intense working period. To raise energy levels. To raise spirits and have some fun.

Directions:

1. Students form one large circle facing inwards and are told to imagine they are going on a horse ride.

2. Teacher mimics the sound of horses' hooves by slapping his/her knees alternately in 'fours'. Everyone joins in and once a rhythm has been established, the teacher leads a change in pace – getting students used to the commands 'gallop faster', 'canter' and 'trot slowly'.

3. The teacher introduces various new commands and actions:

- 'Jump a big fence' – everyone stops slapping and holds their hands in the air until the horse lands again

- 'Jump a little fence' – everyone jumps in the air and shouts 'hup!'

- 'Gallop through water' – slap sides of face

- 'Watch out for Indians' – make 'whooping' noises

- 'Under the whip' – slap self vigorously on behind

Note:

This activity is best suited to groups in which students know each other quite well and work well together. It will result in chaos if used with fragmented groups or with individuals prone to silliness.

Energiser 11:

Sit down if you know

Number of people: Any.

Materials: None required.

Time: 4-5 minutes.

Purpose: To re-focus a group. To provide some light relief following intense working period. To raise energy levels. To raise spirits and have some fun.

Directions:

1. Ask the whole class to stand up.

2. Ask the group a question – start with a fairly difficult question that not many students will know.

3. Direct students to tell someone next to them what they think the answer is, if they can think of one.

4. Tell the group the right answer; those who gave their neighbour the correct answer are allowed to sit.

5. Repeat the procedure a few times until all students are seated. Vary the questions adding off-topic 'fun' questions to make sure less able students aren't singled out.

Notes/variations:

Students stand and take turns to tell the group one thing they have learned from an earlier lesson. That person sits down and the next person does the same. To prevent repetition this can be done in small groups, where students only give their answers to the students in their group.

The standing and sitting can be reversed, and off-topic questions can be included so that students who have difficulty in the subject aren't always the ones left standing.

Energiser 12:

Mini/MAXI Stretches

Number of people: Any.

Materials: None required.

Time: 4-5 minutes.

Purpose: To re-focus a group. To provide some light relief following intense working period. To raise energy levels. To raise spirits and have some fun. This has the benefit of being easy to relate to the lesson content.

Directions:

1. Ask the whole class to stand up.

2. Demonstrate a 'mini' stretch (move a small part of your body: curl a lip, twitch a finger etc) compared with a 'MAXI' stretch (reach for the ceiling, lift a leg etc). Whilst demonstrating the stretch, simultaneously state out loud one fact that is topic-related.

3. Everyone then copies the stretch whilst repeating the same fact and the teacher then nominates another student to model a 'mini' or 'MAXI' stretch whilst stating another   topic-related fact. This student must then call on another to do the same.

4. Perform four or five stretches before continuing with the lesson (or pulling a muscle, whichever is the sooner).

Energiser 13:

Collaborative Countdown

Purpose: To re-focus a group. To provide some light relief following intense working period. To raise energy levels. To build group cohesion and team spirit.

Note: The idea is to count down from 20 to 1 as a group. It sounds easy but what makes it fiendishly difficult and a bit of a riot is that there is absolutely no order for people to follow in calling out the numbers.

Number of people: Whole class.

Materials: N/A.

Time: 10 minutes.

Directions:

1. Ask students to close their eyes then explain the objective – to count down from 20 to 1, as a group.

2. Once you've announced the task there will probably be a moment of confused silence as students wait to be told how to start off. You just look at them a while until they start asking questions.

3. Tell them anyone can start off by shouting out '20' and that once that has happened, the next person to speak must say '19' and so on. Anyone can call out the numbers but if any two people call out the same number at the same time, the game is started again from 20.

Warning: It can get frustrating if the game has to be repeatedly restarted without much progress made, so try to keep the group as relaxed as possible... and be prepared for a tremendous reaction from the group when they eventually achieve a full countdown. They really will see it as quite a group achievement.

Energiser 14:

Ferris Bueller

Purpose: To re-focus a group. To provide some light relief following intense working period. To raise energy levels. To build group cohesion and team spirit.

Note:

The title of this party-type game/energiser doesn't give much away. It reminds me of the scene in the film where Ferris' teacher is trying to determine his whereabouts. 'Anyone seen Bueller? Anyone? Anyone?' You'll see why in a minute.

Number of people: Whole class.

Materials: N/A

Time: 10 minutes.

Directions:

1. Students move their chairs into one big circle, facing inwards, with one person standing in the middle (nominate one if there are no volunteers).

2. The person in the middle asks the rest of the group a question beginning with... 'Anyone...' eg: 'Anyone have eggs for breakfast?', 'Anyone got a pair of Adidas football boots?', 'Anyone been to France on holiday?' . The aim of the asker is to get to sit down.

3. Anyone sitting who can answer 'yes' to the question must jump out of their chair and move to one of the other empty chairs in the circle. At the same time, the person asking the question has to find an empty chair to sit in. The person who doesn't manage to get themselves an empty chair to sit in is the next to ask a question.

Note: Players aren't allowed to sit in the chair next to them and can't return to their own seat, so there is potential for World War III to break out. This could also be a good test of your student management skills.

Obviously, the idea is to ask a question which will get as many people as possible on their feet and swapping chairs. 'Anyone hate school?' usually works.

Energiser 15:

Teacher Says...

Purpose: To re-focus a group. To provide some light relief following intense working period. To raise energy levels and moods. To build group cohesion and team spirit.

Note:

This is an energiser in the purest sense of the word. It will get students on their feet and moving. It will also have you in hysterics.

Number of people: Whole class.

Materials: N/A.

Time: A few minutes occasionally throughout the lesson.

Directions:

1. At any time you feel the class flagging ask everyone to get to their feet. Tell them this is going to be similar to the game 'Simon Says' except that every time you tell them what to do, they have to do it.

2. Shout out walk! and students must walk briskly on the spot – swinging their arms (carefully in small classrooms) as if on a jolly jaunt in the country.

3. Shout stop! and berate anyone who continues to move. Repeat the walk/stop commands until you're sure they've got the hang of things. Then you turn up the heat...

4. 'From now on, when I say stop it means walk and when I say walk it means stop.' Have them practise that a few times, perhaps speeding things up a little just to get them confused.

5. Next, it's time to introduce a couple of other commands – jump and run. 'When I say jump! you jump up and down on the spot and when I say run! – well, I think you can guess what you need to do.

Practice again using all four commands (the reversed walk/stop and jump/run) before unleashing the final head twister – 'From now on, when I say run I mean jump and when I say jump I mean run.'

You can have them falling about in a state of total confusion (or exhaustion) with just those four commands. If they seem to cope, of course, there are always new commands you could bring into the mix (wave, clap, hop, handstand etc).

Warning - all this fun and POWER could lead to thoughts of world domination. If you find yourself wanting to grow a pointy moustache and twiddle the ends while cackling... just relax for a while in the corner, with a nice cuppa.

And Finally!

"It made my naughtiest student as quiet as a mouse!"

"Thank you so much for the superbly wonderful videos! I benefited a lot from your creative secret agent method! It made my naughtiest student as quiet as a mouse! THANK YOU..."

Yasaman Shafiee (Take Control of the Noisy Class customer)

Take Control of The Noisy Class

To get your copy, go here:

https://www.amazon.co.uk/Take-Control-Noisy-Class-Super-effective/dp/1785830082/

Also, if you'd like to receive my FREE **Behaviour Tips** on an inconsistent and irregular basis via my email service, just sign up for your free book resources and you'll start receiving my Behaviour Tips.

http://needsfocusedteaching.com/kindle/fun/

These contain short, practical ideas and strategies for responding to all kinds of inappropriate classroom behaviour, as well as some handy teaching tips and ideas for improving student engagement. All this will be sent direct to your email inbox once or twice a week, along with occasional notifications about some of our other products, special offers etc.

Obviously, you can opt out of this service any time you wish but in our experience, most people pick up a lot of *wonderful* ideas from these emails. And feel free to forward the messages and resources on to other teachers (staff meetings, staff room, pop them into your Christmas cards etc.).

Just remember to look out for emails from '***Needs Focused Teaching***' so that you don't miss all the goodies.

"Thanks a million. As a fresh teacher, I find this invaluable."

"Finally something concrete and applicable in real life – I've had enough of the people who have never set their foot in a real classroom but know how everything should be done in theory. Thanks a million. As a fresh teacher, I find this invaluable."

Jasna (Take Control of the Noisy Class customer)

Final Reminder!

 If you haven't already done so, head on over to the FREE resources page:

http://needsfocusedteaching.com/kindle/fun/

One more thing... Please help me get this book to as many teachers as possible, by leaving an honest review...

"I have seen nothing short of miracles occur."

"I have seen nothing short of miracles occur. My students' attitudes and behaviours have improved; they are excited and personally involved in their educational experience! What more could I ask? My E books have become my bible!!! I truly am a disciple!!!!! Love you guys."

Dawn (NeedsFocusedTeaching customer)

Review Request

If you enjoyed this book, please leave me an honest review! Your support really does matter and it really does make a difference. I do read all the reviews so I can get your feedback and I do make changes as a result of that feedback.

If you'd like to leave a review, then all you need to do is go to the review section on the book's Amazon page. You'll see a big button that states "Write a customer review". Click on that and you're good to go!

You can also use the following links to locate the book on Amazon:

https://www.amazon.com/dp/B074B13NP8

https://www.amazon.co.uk/dp/B074B13NP8

For all other countries, please head over to the relevant Amazon site and either search for the book title or simply copy and paste the following code in the Amazon search bar to be taken directly to the book:

B072MJR85T

Have fun and thanks for your support...

Rob

"...your strategies work wonders!"

"Thank you so much Rob for what you are doing for the profession, your strategies work wonders! I have never tried the 'pen' but will do next time! Seriously speaking, I give the link to your productions to many young teachers I know because they are so unhappy sometimes and they need help which they find with what you do! So, thanks again and carry on with your good job!"

Marie (Take Control of the Noisy Class customer)

Suggested resource providers

Name: HowtoLearn.com and HowtoLearn.teachable.com

Specialty: Personalized Learning Assessments, Learning Solutions, Courses for Teachers, Parents and Students.

Website: www.HowtoLearn.com

Details: Online since 1996, the brainchild of best-selling author and college professor, Pat Wyman, known as America's Most Trusted Learning Expert. We invite you to become part of our global community and closed Facebook group. Your Learning Questions Answered at http://www.HowtoLearn.com/your-learning-questions-answered.

Resources: Take our Free Learning Styles Quiz at HowtoLearn.com and check out parent/teacher tested and approved courses at HowtoLearn.teachable.com.

*   *   *

Name: Time Savers for Teachers (Stevan Krajnjan)

Speciality: Resources guaranteed to save you time.

Website: http://www.timesaversforteachers.com/ashop/affiliate.php?id=7

Details: Popular forms, printable and interactive teacher resources that save time. Stevan Krajnjan was presented with an Exceptional Teacher Award by The Learning Disabilities Association of Mississauga and North Peel in recognition for outstanding work with children who have learning disabilities.

Resources: www.timesaversforteachers.com

* * *

Name: Nicola Morgan (NSM Training & Consultancy).

Speciality: Innovative resources to motivate staff and empower schools.

Website: www.nsmtc.co.uk

Details: NSM Training & Consultancy provides high quality training for teaching/non teaching staff in the UK and internationally. We provide a large range of courses, expert consultancy and guidance, publications, conferences as well as innovative resources to motivate staff and empower schools.

Resources: http://www.nsmtc.co.uk/resources/

* * *

Name: Susan Fitzell

Speciality: Special Education Needs

Website: www.SusanFitzell.com

Details: Seminar Handouts and supplemental resources for Differentiated Instruction, Motivation, Special Education Needs, Co-teaching, and more.

Resources: http://downloads.susanfitzell.com/

* * *

Name: Patricia Hensley

Speciality: Special Education

Website: http://successfulteaching.net

Details: Strategies and ideas for all grade levels. Great resource for new and struggling teachers.

Resources: Free Student Job Description. https://successfulteaching.blogspot.com/2007/10/student-job-description.html

*   *   *

Name: Julia G. Thompson

Speciality: Educational consultant, writer, and presenter.

Website: www.juliagthompson.com.

Details: Author of The First-Year Teacher's Survival Guide, Julia G Thompson specializes in assisting new teachers learn to thrive in their new profession.

Resources: For 57 free forms and templates to make your school year easier, just click go to her website and click on the Professional Binder page

*   *   *

Name: Steve Reifman

Speciality: Teaching the Whole Child (Empowering Classroom Management & Improving Student Learning)

Website: www.stevereifman.com

Details: National Board Certified Elementary Teacher & Amazon Best-Selling Author.

Author of '10 Steps to Empowering Classroom Management: Build a Productive, Cooperative Culture Without Using Rewards'

Resources: https://www.youtube.com/user/sreifman (FREE, 1-2 minute videos with tips for teachers & parents)

* * *

Name: Dave Vizard

Speciality: Behaviour Management

Website: www.behavioursolutions.com

Details: Creator of Brain Break materials and Ways to Manage Challenging Behaviour ebook.

Resources: www.behavioursolutions.myshopify.com/pages/brain-breaks

* * *

Name: Marjan Glavac

Specialty: Tips on getting a teaching job (resume, cover letter, interviews); classroom management strategies.

Website: www.thebusyeducator.com

Details: Marjan Glavac is a best selling motivational author, engaging speaker and elementary classroom teacher with over 29 years of teaching experience.

Resources: Free weekly newsletter, 4 free eBooks (http://thebusyeducator.com/homepage.htm)

* * *

Name: Dr. Rich Allen

Specialty: Workshops and keynotes on engagement strategies for students of all ages

Website: greenlighteducation.net

Details: Author of 'Green Light Teaching' and 'The Rock 'n Roll Classroom'

Resources: Please join our Teaching tips community and access lots of free resources and ideas for your classroom by clicking HERE.

* * *

Name: Ross Morrison McGill

Speciality: Managing director at TeacherToolkit Ltd.

Website: https://www.teachertoolkit.co.uk/

Details: Ross Morrison McGill is a deputy headteacher working in an inner-city school in North London. He is the Most Followed Teacher on Twitter in the UK and writes the Most Influential Blog on Education in the UK.

Resources: https://www.amazon.co.uk/Ross-Morrison-McGill/e/B00G33GTEO/ref=dp_byline_cont_book_1

What people say about us

"Even if you have never had "the class from hell", there is something here for you"

"As a PGCE student it is great to have the opportunity to pick up user-friendly and easily accessible information. The 'Behaviour Needs' course provides exactly that. In a series of amusing, creative, fast-paced sections, Rob Plevin builds up a staggering amount of practical and thought provoking material on classroom behaviour management. All of which are easily translated back in the classroom. Even if you have never had "the class from hell", there is something here for you and the follow up information from the website is laden with golden nuggets which will give you loads more ideas and interventions."

Steve Edwards (Workshop Attendee and Take Control of the Noisy Class customer)

* * *

"I want you to know that you have changed the lives of 40 of my students."

"What an informative day. The sessions on positive reinforcement and the importance of relationships were particularly memorable. I want you to know that you have changed the lives of 40 of my students. Thank you!"

Joanne W. (Singapore Workshop Attendee)

* * *

"...We will be inviting Rob back on every possible occasion to work with all of our participants and trainees."

"We were delighted to be able to get Rob Plevin in to work with our Teach First participants. From the start his dynamic approach captivated the group and they were enthralled throughout. Rob covered crucial issues relating to behaviour management thoroughly and worked wonders in addressing the participants' concerns about teaching in some of the most challenging schools in the country. We will be inviting Rob back on every possible occasion to work with all of our participants and trainees."

Terry Hudson, (Regional Director 'Teach First', Sheffield Hallam University)

* * *

"Thank you for helping me to be in more control."

"Rob, thank you very much for sharing your experience and reminding of these simple but effective things to do. Students' behaviour (or actually my inability to control it) is so frustrating that at times it feels that nothing can help. Thank you for helping me to be in more control."

Natasha Grydasova (_Take Control of the Noisy Class_ customer)

* * *

"I am HAPPILY spending my Sat afternoon listening, watching and reading all your extremely helpful information!"

"Thank You Rob! What a wealth of excellent ideas! This is my 30th year teaching! You would think after 30 years teaching that I wouldn't need to be viewing your awesome videos and reading your helpful blog and website. However, I am HAPPILY spending my Sat afternoon listening, watching and reading all your extremely helpful information! Thank You So Much! I will be one of your biggest fans from now on!"

Kelly Turk (_Needs Focused Video Pack_ customer)

* * *

"...terrific for those teachers who are frustrated."

"Great easy-to-listen-to video tips that will be terrific for those teachers who are frustrated.

I'm forwarding this email on to the principals in my district right away!"

Sumner price (Take Control of the Noisy Class customer)

* * *

"Many thanks for all these really helpful life-savers!"

"Very many thanks. I have given myself trouble by letting kids into the room in a restless state with inevitable waste of teaching time. Your advice on calming them down in a positive, non-confrontational way and building rapport is very timely. Many thanks for all these really helpful life-savers!"

Philip Rozario (Take Control of the Noisy Class customer)

* * *

"Fantastic way to create a calm and secure learning environment for all the students."

"Thanks so much Rob. Fantastic way to create a calm and secure learning environment for all the students. It's great how you model the way we should interact with the students – firmly but always with respect."

Marion (Take Control of the Noisy Class customer)

* * *

"I will be recommending that the teachers in training that I deal with should have a look at these videos."

These tips and hints are put in a really clear, accessible fashion. As coordinator of student teachers in my school, I will be recommending that the teachers in training that I deal with should have a look at these videos.

Deb (Take Control of the Noisy Class customer)

* * *

"I found Rob Plevin's workshop just in time to save me from giving up."

"I found Rob Plevin's workshop just in time to save me from giving up. It should be compulsory – everybody in teaching should attend a Needs-Focused workshop and meet the man with such a big heart who will make you see the important part you can play in the lives of your most difficult students."

Heather Beames (Workshop Attendee)

* * *

"...the ideas, strategies and routines shared with our teachers have led to improved classroom practice."

"The Needs Focused Behaviour Management workshops in support of teacher training in Northern Ireland have been very well received and the ideas, strategies and routines shared with our teachers have led to improved classroom practice. This has been validated by both inspections at the University and observations of teachers."

Celia O'Hagan, (PGCE Course Leader, School of Education, University of Ulster)

* * *

"I have never enjoyed a course, nor learnt as much as I did with Rob."

"What a wonderfully insightful, non-patronising, entertainingly informative day. I have never enjoyed a course, nor learnt as much as I did with Rob. I was so impressed that I am recommending our school invite Rob along to present to all the staff so that we can all benefit from his knowledge, experience and humour."

Richard Lawson-Ellis (Workshop Attendee)

* * *

"...since I started following the principles in your materials, I have seen a vast improvement."

"Hi Rob, I would just like to say that since I started following the principles in your materials, I have seen a vast improvement. I had to teach a one hour interview lesson yesterday and was told that they thought the lesson was super and they loved my enthusiasm! I got the job!

Diane Greene (_Take Control of the Noisy Class customer_)

* * *

"Thanks to you, students from 30 some schools are truly engaged and not throwing pencils at the sub!"

*Rob, Your student engagement series has been out of this world. I've already used various techniques as a substitute and students said I was **the best sub ever.** Thanks to you, students from 30 some schools are truly engaged and not throwing pencils at the sub!"*

Leslie Mueller (Student Engagement Formula customer)

* * *

"So often professional development training is a waste of time; you may get one little gem from a whole day of training. You've given numerous strategies in 5 minutes."

Wow! So many people have gained so much from your videos! Teachers are time poor. A quick grab of effective ideas is what we all need. So often professional development training is a waste of time; you may get one little gem from a whole day of training. You've given numerous strategies in 5 minutes. Thanks for your generosity.

Mary – Ann (Take Control of the Noisy Class customer)

Strategies List

Made in the USA
Middletown, DE
25 March 2018